84 CHARING CROSS ROAD

Based on the book by Helene Hanff

Adapted by James Roose-Evans

‖SAMUEL FRENCH‖

samuelfrench.co.uk

THINKING ABOUT PERFORMING A SHOW?

There are thousands of plays and musicals available to perform from Samuel French right now, and applying for a licence is easier and more affordable than you might think

---

From classic plays to brand new musicals, from monologues to epic dramas, there are shows for everyone.

Plays and musicals are protected by copyright law so if you want to perform them, the first thing you'll need is a licence. This simple process helps support the playwright by ensuring they get paid for their work, and means that you'll have the documents you need to stage the show in public.

Not all our shows are available to perform all the time, so it's important to check and apply for a licence before you start rehearsals or commit to doing the show.

LEARN MORE & FIND THOUSANDS OF SHOWS

Browse our full range of plays and musicals and find out more about how to license a show

www.samuelfrench.co.uk/perform

Talk to the friendly experts in our Licensing team for advice on choosing a show, and help with licensing

plays@samuelfrench.co.uk   020 7387 9373

Acting Editions

BORN TO PERFORM

Playscripts designed from the ground up to work the way you do in rehearsal, performance and study

---

Larger, clearer text for easier reading

Wider margins for notes

Performance features such as character and props lists, sound and lighting cues, and more

---

+ CHOOSE A SIZE AND STYLE TO SUIT YOU

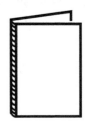

STANDARD EDITION

Our regular paperback book at our regular size

SPIRAL-BOUND EDITION

The same size as the Standard Edition, but with a sturdy, easy-to-fold, easy-to-hold spiral-bound spine

LARGE EDITION

A4 size and spiral bound, with larger text and a blank page for notes opposite every page of text. Perfect for technical and directing use

---

LEARN MORE | samuelfrench.co.uk/actingeditions

**Other plays by James Roose-Evans
published and licensed by Samuel French**

Cider with Rosie

**FIND PERFECT PLAYS TO PERFORM AT
www.samuelfrench.co.uk/perform**

ABOUT THE AUTHOR

Helene's parents were both passionate theatre-goers. Her father had wanted to run away from college to go on the stage as a song and dance man. After two years he got stranded in Montana, wired home for money and his grandmother sent him a train ticket instead. When he came home he had lice and his grandmother threw him into the bath-tub, burned all his clothes, and told him he was through with theatre! So he became a shirt salesman, married and settled down in Philadelphia, which was a favourite try-out city for Broadway shows. He would swap shirts for free tickets!

So, as Helene said, "throughout the Depression, though the taxes on our house weren't paid, or the instalments on the old second-hand car, and though the prescription for my mother's new glasses went unfilled, every Monday night the Hanff family: father, mother, Helene and her two older brothers, all went to the theatre!"

James Roose-Evans's first impression on meeting Helene at the Garrick Club: "diminutive, in a black trouser suit, with silk blouse and cravat, her short, cropped hair framing the monkey-like face, she speaks in sharp, shooting phrases, like a small boy who, dressed as a cowboy, fires off toy pistols with glee. She is like a showbiz kid performing to entertain the adults. One senses, however, that this wise-cracking is simply her way of getting by, of surviving."

Underneath is a melancholy and loneliness.

At lunch, as she eats, she smokes: a mouthful of food, then a drag at her cigarette; another mouthful, another drag. The head waiter whispers to me, "You do realise, sir, that smoking is not permitted in the Coffee Room before 2.30?" "Yes," I reply, "but you try telling that to Miss Hanff!"

AUTHOR'S NOTE

For twenty years, from 1949, when she was thirty-two, until 1969, a struggling New York writer named Helene Hanff and the staff at the London antiquarian bookshop Marks & Co carried on a remarkable correspondence. It began with an innocent enquiry about fine book editions, but continued for two decades. Their letters, encompassing a period that went from Churchill's war to the Beatles's invasion, became a chronicle of an era as well as a record of a deep friendship.

84 Charing Cross Road is James Roose-Evans's unique adaptation for the stage of this cross-Atlantic correspondence, which he revised and developed further for the 2011–12 production. On a stage divided between Miss Hanff's cluttered New York apartment and the inviting mustiness of the Marks & Co bookshop, we watch as Miss Hanff and her friends "read" their letters, revealing beneath mundane book orders and witty literary repartee, their personal lives, and a warmth and caring that distance could not diminish. As one reviewer wrote, "It all seems so simple, just a collection of letters between people linked by their common love for books, but by the time you reach the end you will have looked into their hearts and shared the richness of their relationship."

MUSIC USE NOTE

Licensees are solely responsible for obtaining formal written permission from copyright owners to use copyrighted music in the performance of this play and are strongly cautioned to do so. If no such permission is obtained by the licensee, then the licensee must use only original music that the licensee owns and controls. Licensees are solely responsible and liable for all music clearances and shall indemnify the copyright owners of the play(s) and their licensing agent, Samuel French, against any costs, expenses, losses and liabilities arising from the use of music by licensees. Please contact the appropriate music licensing authority in your territory for the rights to any incidental music.

USE OF COPYRIGHT MUSIC

A licence issued by Samuel French Ltd to perform this play does not include permission to use the incidental music specified in this copy.

Where the place of performance is already licensed by the PERFORMING RIGHT SOCIETY (PRS) a return of the music used must be made to them. If the place of performance is not so licensed then application should be made to the PRS, 2 Pancras Square, London, N1C 4AG.

A separate and additional licence from PHONOGRAPHIC PERFORMANCE LTD, 1 Upper James Street, London W1F 9DE (www.ppluk.com) is needed whenever commercial recordings are used.

IMPORTANT BILLING AND CREDIT REQUIREMENTS

If you have obtained performance rights to this title, please refer to your licensing agreement for important billing and credit requirements.

This revival production of *84 Charing Cross Road* ran at Salisbury Playhouse from 5 February 2015 and subsequently at Cambridge Arts Theatre from 2 September 2016. The cast (in alphabetical order) was as follows:

Megan Wells / Maxine Stuart	Lysette Anthony
Joan Todd	Jemma Churchill
Helene Hanff	Janie Dee
Frank Doel	Clive Francis
Cecily Farr	Alice Haig
Mr Martin	Ted Merwood
William Humphries	Samuel Townsend

Director: James Roose-Evans
Assistant Director: Martin Parr
Designer: Norman Coates
Lighting: Peter Hunter
Sound: John Leonard

CHARACTERS

HELENE

FRANK

ALVIN

CECILY

MR MARTIN

MAXINE

MEGAN

BILL

MRS TODD

PILOT

ACT I

The set comprises the shop, which takes up two thirds of the stage, and HELENE's *apartment, which occupies the remaining third of the space.*

The floor in front of HELENE's *desk is littered with screwed-up balls of typing paper, discarded efforts. Later she will tidy these up. Her apartment is cluttered, and there are orange crate bookshelves, a board for pinning up cards, mementos and cuttings.*

At no time during the play does the actress playing HELENE *have eye contact with the other actors or they with her. The occupants of the shop act in a naturalistic style when interacting among themselves, but when in communication with* HELENE *they must be acutely aware of her, and she of them, but never looking directly at each other.*

There are books everywhere, all over the floor, as well as on the shelves. There are mounds of catalogues, old torn books, ephemera of all kinds.

The table centre stage is set aside for especially rare old books, which are handled with care. Most of the stock will be leather-bound and of quality.

The lights come up first on the shop where CECILY *is standing on a stepladder looking for a book.* FRANK *is upstage going through the order book, and* MEGAN *at one point will enter with mail for him, one letter of which is the one from* HELENE.

Through the windows of the shop – with books displayed on shelves – we can glimpse the street outside. A sign which reads "CLOSED" on one side and "OPEN" on the other hangs on the glass-panelled door of the shop, and there are the usual prints clipped to a string across the door.

Far upstage is a recess with a desk where **MR MARTIN** *works, and also* **MEGAN**. *There is an old-fashioned telephone on this desk.*

On the other side of the stage **HELENE** *is smoking and reading a copy of* The Saturday Review of Literature, *where she notes details of Marks & Co and begins to type.*

HELENE Apartment 1a, 14 East 95th Street, New York City, New York, October 5th 1949, to Marks and Company, 84 Charing Cross Road, London WC2. England!

FRANK *is now moving downstage to his desk with* **HELENE**'s *first letter to him.*

Gentlemen! Your ad in *The Saturday Review of Literature...*

FRANK *slits open her letter with a paper knife, looks at the address and reads.*

says that you specialise in out-of-print books.

The phrase "antiquarian booksellers" scares me somewhat, as I equate "antique" with "expensive". I am a poor writer with an antiquarian taste in books and all the things I want are impossible to get over here except in very expensive rare editions or in Barnes and Noble's grimy marked-up schoolboy copies.

I enclose a list of my most pressing problems.

FRANK *hands the list to* **MEGAN**, *who beckons* **CECILY**, *who goes to look for the Bibles.*

If you have any clean second-hand copies of any of the books on the list, for no more than five dollars each, will you consider this a purchase order and send them to me. Very truly yours...

MEGAN *looks up as though to register the name.*

Helene Hanff. *(Pause) Miss* Helene Hanff.

CECILY *now has two Bibles in her hand but is searching for others.*

FRANK Dear Madam: In reply to your letter of October 5th we have managed to clear up two thirds of your problem.

MEGAN *crosses to him with the Hazlitt and Stevenson.*

The three Hazlitt essays you want are contained in the *Nonesuch Press* edition of his selected essays, and the Stevenson is found in *Virginibus Puerisque.* We are sending nice copies of both these by book post...

Having checked them, he lets MEGAN *take them upstage to prepare an invoice.*

And we trust that they will arrive safely in due course and that you will be pleased with them.

BILL *enters. He stands beside her as she completes the invoice, which she slips inside the top book and hands to him to take out to parcel up in the outer office.*

The Leigh Hunt essays are not going to be so easy but we will see if we can find an attractive volume with them all in.

CECILY *is now standing at his side with an armful of Bibles, and he will select the one he wants. She then replaces the unwanted Bibles.*

We haven't the Latin Bible you describe but we have a Latin New Testament, also a Greek New Testament, ordinary modern editions in cloth binding. Would you like these?

MR MARTIN *enters. He shows* FRANK *two books he has acquired from a sale, and then takes* MEGAN'*s place at desk area upstage, where she was standing in for him. She sits at centre table, examining a book.* CECILY *exits.*

On HELENE'*s side of the stage her door bell rings and she goes to answer, calling out before hand, "Who is it?" and a voice comes back, "It's Alvin, Miss Hanff".*

She opens the door and takes the package from the unseen porter.

ALVIN   *(offstage)* A parcel of books arrived for you, Miss Hanff – all the way from Great Britain!

HELENE   Oh, thanks Alvin, thanks for dropping them off.

ALVIN   No problem, Miss Hanff. A real pleasure.

In the shop, while HELENE *unwraps the parcel, the telephone rings and* MR MARTIN *deals with the call. The date is November 3rd 1949.*

HELENE   Gentlemen! The books arrived safely. The Robert Louis Stevenson is so fine it embarrasses my orange crate bookshelves. I'm almost afraid to handle such soft vellum and heavy cream-coloured pages. Being used to the dead-white paper and stiff cardboard-y covers of American books, I never knew a book could be such a joy to touch.

She puts down the STEVENSON *and crosses to her sofa to get her handbag. She removes six dollars from her purse.*

A Britisher, whose girl lives upstairs, translated the one pound seventeen and sixpence for me and says I owe you five dollars and thirty cents for the two books. I hope he got it right. I enclose a five-dollar bill and a single...

She has taken an airmail envelope and is putting the dollars inside.

Please use the seventy cents towards the price of the New Testaments, both of which I want. Will you please translate your prices hereafter? I don't add too well in plain American and I haven't a prayer of ever mastering bilingual arithmetic!

She licks the envelope flap.

Yours, Helene Hanff.

She seals the envelope and is about to drop it in her 'box' when a thought strikes her.

P.S. I hope "Madam" doesn't mean over there what it means here!

She drops the letter into her 'box'.

FRANK Dear Miss Hanff! We are very happy you liked the Stevenson so much...

MEGAN *looks up and moves towards* FRANK.

We are sending off the New Testaments, with an invoice listing the amount due in both pounds and dollars...

He is handing the Bibles to MEGAN.

And we hope you will be pleased with them.

Your six dollars arrived safely...

MEGAN *is moving away but on the "six dollars", she stops and turns back to take the dollars from* FRANK. *They exchange a comic look of despair.* MEGAN *then hands the dollars to* MR MARTIN, *who looks at them with curiosity, as also does* CECILY, *who returns at this moment.* CECILY *takes the two books from* MEGAN, *who has made out an invoice, standing at the table beside*

MR MARTIN *to do this.* **MEGAN** *then returns to centre table and* **CECILY** *exits.*

But we should feel very much easier if you would send your remittance by postal order in future, as this would be quite a bit safer for you than entrusting dollar bills in the mails. Yours faithfully, F.P.D. *(Pause)* For Marks & Company.

HELENE *rises and moves to front of desk with the Bible.*

What kind of a black Protestant Bible is this? Kindly inform the Church of England they have loused up the most beautiful prose ever written. Whoever told them to tinker with the Vulgate Latin? They'll burn for it, you mark my words! It's nothing to me, I'm Jewish myself. But I have a Catholic sister-in-law, a Methodist sister-in-law, and a whole raft of Presbyterian cousins (through my Great-Uncle Abraham, who converted) and an aunt who's a Christian Science healer, and I like to think none of them would countenance this Anglican Latin Bible if they knew it existed. As it happens, they don't know Latin existed.

MR MARTIN *exits.*

Well, the hell with it. I've been using my Latin teacher's Vulgate, what I imagine I'll do is just not give it back till you find me one of my own.

She takes four dollars out of her purse, takes an airmail envelope and puts dollars inside.

I enclose four dollars to cover the three dollars eighty-eight cents due to you, buy yourself a cup of coffee with the twelve cents. There's no post office near here and I'm not running all the way to Rockefeller Plaza to stand in line for a three-dollar-88-cents money order. If I wait till I get down there for something else, I won't have the three dollars eighty-eight cents any more. I have implicit faith in the US Airmail and His Majesty's Postal Service.

*She puts the letter in the 'box' then checks her notebook
at the side of her typewriter.*

Have you got a copy of Landor's *Imaginary Conversations*?

MEGAN *looks up at this.*

I think there are several volumes. The one I want is with
the Greek Conversations.

There is in fact a set of Landors on the table at which
MEGAN *sits. She picks up one, consults it. Takes another,
checks the contents – yes, it is the one with the Aesop
and Rhodope conversations. She brings it to* FRANK.

If it contains a dialogue between Aesop and Rhodope
that'll be the one I want. Yours, Helene Hanff.

She seals envelope and drops it into the 'box'.

FRANK   Dear Miss Hanff: Your four dollars arrived safely
and we have credited the twelve cents to your account.

MEGAN *now hands the volume to* FRANK. *He checks it,
and then takes it, handing the dollars to* MEGAN.

We happen to have in stock Volume Two of the *Works and
Life of Walter Savage Landor,* which contains the Greek
dialogues, including the ones mentioned in your letter, as
well as the Roman dialogues. It is an old edition, published
in 1876, not very handsome but well bound and a good clean
copy, and we are sending it off today with invoice enclosed.

He has moved upstage and handed the book to MEGAN,
who makes out an invoice. He turns back.

I am sorry we made the mistake with the Latin Bible and
will try to find a Vulgate for you. Not forgetting the Leigh
Hunt. Yours faithfully, F.P.D. *(pause)* For Marks & Company.

HELENE   December 8th 1949.

Sir: Well, it feels witless to keep writing "Gentlemen" when the same solitary soul is obviously taking care of everything for me.

FRANK *reacts to this. He stands at the side of his desk, reading a catalogue.*

Savage Landor arrived safely and promptly fell open to a Roman dialogue where two cities have just been destroyed by war and everybody was being crucified and begging passing Roman soldiers to run them through and end the agony. It'll be a relief to turn to Aesop and Rhodope, where all you have to worry about is a famine.

I do love second-hand books that open to the page some previous owner read most often.

The day Hazlitt came he opened to a page that said, "I hate to read new books" and I hollered, "Comrade!" I enclose a dollar...

FRANK *looks up at this.* **HELENE** *finds an envelope and places it inside.*

which Brian, British boyfriend of Kay upstairs, says will cover the eight shillings I owe you, you forgot to translate!

She moves to front of desk. **FRANK** *is quietly at work.*

Now then! Brian told me you are all rationed to two ounces of meat per family per week and one egg per person per month, and I am simply appalled.

She ferrets among a pile of scripts on the floor and finds the catalogue. She squats or kneels.

He has a catalogue from a British firm here that flies food from Denmark to his mother in England, so I am sending a small Christmas present to Marks & Company. I hope there will be enough to go round.

I am sending it care of you, F.P.D. – whoever you are!

*Music of "**JINGLE BELLS**". The others enter on the word "sending", led by* **MEGAN**, *who holds a large cardboard box covered with customs labels. They approach* **FRANK**, *smiling, and set the box on the table at the side of his desk.*

Noel, Helene Hanff!

Music swells. **FRANK** *takes scissors and cuts the string. They open the parcel, and brightly coloured parcels, in Christmas wrapping, emerge: (two tins of pork sausages, tins of bacon, of cheese, a tinned cake, a packet of dried eggs, and tins of jam.)*

Then, on cue, **MEGAN** *lifts out a large tin of ham.*

F.P.D! Crisis! I sent that package off. The chief item in it was a six-pound ham. I figured you could take it to the butcher and get it sliced up so everybody would have some to take home. But then I've just noticed on your invoice...

The actors freeze, looking front, as though listening to **HELENE**.

it says, "B. Marks, M. Cohen, Proprietors". *Are they Kosher?* I could rush over a tongue. *Advise please!*

They all laugh.

FRANK Dear Miss Hanff: Just a note to let you know that your gift parcel arrived safely and the contents have been shared out between the staff. Mr Marks and Mr Cohen insisted that we divide it up among ourselves and not include the bosses.

Music out. **CECILY** *exits with box, and* **BILL** *follows* **MR MARTIN** *out.* **MEGAN** *goes to* **MR MARTIN**'s *table, holding her share of the parcel.* **FRANK** *places a tin of jam, only the top of the wrapping torn off, on his desk.*

I should just like to add that everything in the parcel was something that either we have never seen or can only be had through the black market. It was extremely kind of you to think of us in this way and we are all extremely grateful. We all wish to express our thanks and send our greetings and best wishes for 1950. Yours faithfully, Frank Doel.

He turns to exit.

HELENE Frank Doel!

FRANK For Marks and Company!

He exits, pausing en route to show **MEGAN** *his present.* **HELENE** *continues working. She puts a piece of paper in the machine and types.*

MEGAN *exits.*

Light change, spring 1950.

HELENE *looks up from her typing.*

HELENE Frank Doel? *(pause, sound of a New York siren.)* Frank Doel?

She pulls the paper out of the machine in despair, screws it up and throws it on the floor. She rises.

Frank Doel, what are you *doing* over there, you are not doing *any*thing, you are just sitting *around*!

FRANK *enters from the outer office, holding* **HELENE**'s *latest letter. He hurries to his desk for a paper knife and opens it. He throws the envelope in the wastepaper basket. He reads the letter with secretive delight.*

HELENE Where is Leigh Hunt? Where is the Oxford *Verse?* Where is the Vulgate and dear goofy John Henry Newman? I thought they'd be such nice uplifting reading for Lent, and *nothing* do you send me. You leave me sitting here, writing long margin notes in library books that don't belong to me; some day they'll find out I did it and take my library card away.

MEGAN *appears from behind the shelves.* HELENE *picks up a catalogue.*

I have made arrangements with the Easter Bunny to bring you an egg.

FRANK *looks up, entertained by this thought.*

He will get over there and find you have died of *inertia.*

HELENE *is removing her woollen jacket and drapes it around her chair. She moves downstage of her desk, she is at a low point.*

I require a book of love poems with spring coming on. No Keats or Shelley, send me poets who can make love without lobbering – Wyatt or Johnson or somebody, use your judgement. Just a nice book, preferably small enough to stick in a slacks pocket and take to Central Park.

Music for "EASTER PARADE" is heard.

FRANK *stands, musing.*

Well, don't just stand there! Go find it! I swear I don't know how that shop keeps going!

She starts to sing "IN YOUR EASTER BONNET" as the music swells, and types. BILL, MR MARTIN *and* CECILY *appear with another parcel.* MEGAN, *at her table, snips the string with a pair of scissors.* FRANK *is watching.* MEGAN *joins the others in bringing the parcel to him. They bring out Easter eggs, boxes of shelled eggs and an absurd duck with a label round its neck. It's a jokey present from* HELENE. MEGAN *reads the label and looks at* FRANK. *He indicates "For me?" and* MEGAN *then hands him the duck, which he places on his desk.*

HELENE *has stopped singing but the music swells.* FRANK *speaks over it, laughing.*

FRANK Dear Miss Hanff: I have to thank you for the very welcome Easter parcel, which arrived safely. We were all delighted to see the tins and the box of shelled eggs, and the rest of the staff join me in thanking you...

They all turn towards him, holding their gifts and he conducts them like a chorus.

ALL For your very kind and generous thoughts of us!

They exit.

FRANK I'm sorry we haven't been able to send any of the books you want.

Softly, from outside in the street, a barrel organ is heard. **FRANK** *is collecting his hat from the hat stand, picks up his umbrella and briefcase, and the box of shelled eggs.*

About the book of love poems, now and then we do get such a volume as you describe. We have none in stock at present but shall look out for one for you. Again, many thanks for the parcel.

CECILY *enters with letters, but stops abruptly when she sees* **FRANK**, *and goes to the stepladder and pretends to be looking for a book.* **MEGAN** *is no longer onstage.*

Faithfully yours, Frank Doel. *(pause)* For Marks & Company.

Exits, traffic noise, door closes, silence.

CECILY *slips to the window to check* **FRANK** *has really gone, and then comes down front. She is holding a clipboard and the letter she has written to* **HELENE**.

CECILY Dear Miss Hanff!

HELENE *looks up at this new voice.*

Please don't let Frank know I'm writing this but every time I send you a bill I've been dying to slip in a little note, and he might not think it quite proper of me. That sounds stuffy and he's not, he's quite nice really, very nice in fact, it's just that he does rather look on you as his private correspondent, as all your letters and parcels are addressed to him. But I just thought I would write to you on my own.

We all love your letters and try to imagine what you must be like. I've decided you're young and very sophisticated and smart-looking.

HELENE *makes a rueful moue at this remark.*

Old Mr Martin thinks you must be quite studious-looking in spite of your wonderful sense of humour. Why don't you send us a snapshot?

HELENE *covers her face.* CECILY *crosses and stands behind* FRANK's *desk.*

If you're curious about Frank—

HELENE *looks up at this, removing spectacles.*

he's in his early forties, quite nice-looking, married to a very sweet Irish girl. I believe she's his second wife. They have two daughters.

She looks at the toy duck and holds it in her arms.

Everyone was so grateful for the parcel. My little ones – girl five, boy four – were in heaven.

With the raisins and eggs I was able to make them a cake! I hope you don't mind my writing.

She quietly puts the duck back.

Please don't mention it when you write to Frank.

With best wishes, Cecily Farr.

MR MARTIN *enters at back.*

MR MARTIN Mrs Farr! About these invoices here...

CECILY Just coming, Mr Martin.

P.S. I shall put my home address on the back in case you should ever want anything from London.

MR MARTIN Mrs Farr!

CECILY Coming, Mr Martin!

She exits.

HELENE, *rising, hands in pockets, is intrigued by this new development.*

HELENE Dear Cecily, Tell Mr Martin I'm so unstudious I never went to college. I just happen to have peculiar tastes in books, thanks to a Cambridge professor named Quiller-Couch, known as Q, whom I fell over in a library when I was seventeen. And I'm about as smart-looking as a Broadway panhandler.

She moves behind her desk, picks up her woollen jacket, then moves back to front of desk, putting it on, rolling the sleeves over her hands, and shivering.

I live in moth-eaten sweaters and wool slacks; they don't give us any heat here in the daytime. It's a five-storey brownstone, and all the other tenants go out to work at nine a.m. and don't come home until six.

She shouts the following offstage, opening her door.

AND WHY SHOULD THE LANDLORD HEAT THE BUILDING FOR ONE SMALL SCRIPT READER-STROKE-WRITER WORKING AT HOME ON THE GROUND FLOOR?

(aside) I bet he's got heat in his apartment!

She closes her door.

CECILY *enters with the mail, reading* **HELENE**'s *letter to her.*

By now **HELENE** *is back at her desk, ready for a morning's work, as she leans forward, elbows on desk.*

Poor Frank! I give him such a hard time. I'm always bawling him out for something. I'm only teasing, but I know he takes me seriously. I keep trying to puncture that proper British reserve. If he gets ulcers, I did it!

Please write and tell me about London. I can't wait for the day when I step off the boat train and feel its dirty sidewalks under my feet. I want to walk up Berkeley Square and down Wimpole Street and stand in St Paul's, where John Donne preached, and sit on the step Elizabeth sat on when she refused to enter the Tower, and like that.

When I go to England, I'll be looking for the England of English Literature!

FRANK *enters from the street, carrying his briefcase and umbrella, and overhears* **CECILY** *reading the end of her letter from* **HELENE**.

Regards, Helene Hanff.

CECILY *guiltily crosses to table centre, dropping several letters en route. She hurries off upstage, bumping into* **MR MARTIN**, *who enters at that moment.* **MR MARTIN** *turns, looks after her, shaking his head before sitting at his desk.*

FRANK *is carrying two books, one of which is wrapped in tissue paper. He looks at* **CECILY** *and at* **MR MARTIN**. *Then goes straight to his desk.*

FRANK Dear Miss Hanff: It is such a long time since we wrote to you and I hope you do not think we have forgotten all about your wants.

He puts down his briefcase at the side of his desk.

Anyway, I have now managed to find for you the *Oxford Book of English Verse*, printed on India paper, original blue cloth binding, 1905, inscription in ink on the fly-leaf, but a good second-hand copy, price two dollars.

MEGAN *enters, reading a letter from a customer. She checks along the shelves for the book required.*

We thought we had better quote before sending, in case you already have purchased a copy.

He puts down the OUP book and handles the book wrapped in tissue paper. He moves front of desk to centre stage.

Some time ago you asked us for Newman's *Idea of a University*. Would you be interested in a first edition? Price six dollars.

He holds out the book teasingly.

HELENE *stares front, mesmerised. The bait has been taken!*

In case you would like them, we will put both books on one side until you have time to reply.

HELENE *rises in a state of high excitement, snatching her handbag from the sofa, then searching for money hidden, squirrel-like, in tins on her desk, in a mug, wherever. She shovels the dollars into an envelope.*

HELENE He has a first edition of Newman's *Idea of a University* for six bucks, do I want it? Dear Frank, yes, I want it!

FRANK *looks up and grins, then takes both books and hands them to **MR MARTIN**.*

I won't be fit to live with myself. I've never cared about first editions per se, but a first edition of that book, oh, my! I can just see it!

More activity among the tins.

Send the Oxford *Verse* too. Never wonder if I found something somewhere else any more. Why should I run all the way to Seventeenth Street, to buy dirty, badly made books when I can buy clean, beautiful ones from you without leaving the typewriter? From where I sit, London's a lot closer than Seventeenth Street...

CECILY *enters from upstage left.*

She hesitates, then sits at table downstage, next to FRANK's *desk. She is pretending to read a book.* MEGAN, *who entered earlier, is standing at the shelves upstage, reading, but quietly observing* CECILY.

HELENE *stuffing dollars into envelope:*

Enclosed, please God, please find eight dollars. Did I tell you about Brian? He buys physics tomes from a technical bookshop in London.

He bought an expensive set and went to Rockefeller Plaza and stood in line and got a money order and cabled it or whatever you do with it. He's a business man, he does things right.

He's not sloppy and haphazard like me.

The money order got lost in transit! Up His Majesty's Postal Service!

She drops the letter into the 'box'.

CECILY *looks up, and brings out from the cover of the book she is pretending to read an envelope and some snapshots.* HELENE *will have an identical set of these photos.*

CECILY Dear Helene: I brought the enclosed snapshots to the shop with me weeks ago, but we have been frightfully busy so have had no chance to send them. They were taken in Norfolk where Doug (my husband) is stationed with the RAF.

MEGAN, *who is anxious for* **CECILY**, *over hears this.*

None of them are very flattering of me but they are the best we have of the children and the one of Doug alone is very good.

HELENE *is looking at the snapshots.* **MEGAN**, *turning a page of her book, crosses slowly to* **FRANK**'s *desk.*

My dear, I do hope you get your wish to come to England. Why not save your pennies and come to England next summer? Mummy and Daddy have a house in Middlesex and would be delighted to put you up.

HELENE *rises thoughtfully, moving front, considering this.*

Megan Wells (**CECILY** *looks across at* **MEGAN** *and they smile.*) and I are going on a week's holiday to Jersey in July. Megan is secretary to the bosses. Why don't you come with us and then you could economise the rest of the month in Middlesex.

During the last sentence **MR MARTIN** *has risen with the ledger and is about to ask* **MEGAN** *a question but notices* **CECILY**, *gossiping as it seems.* **MEGAN** *at once tries to distract his attention, signalling "Beware!" to* **CECILY**, *and guides* **MR MARTIN** *upstage.*

Mr Martin is trying to see what I am writing so I shall have to close. Sincerely, Cecily.

FRANK *enters in a hurry with* **HELENE**'s *latest letter but his way is blocked by* **MEGAN** *and* **MR MARTIN**. *They part. At the same time* **CECILY**, *her head down, is hurrying out and collides with them. She exits.* **MR MARTIN** *again shakes his head at her: he'll have to speak to her, so he follows her out.*

MR MARTIN Mrs Farr, really!

MEGAN *returns with her book to the bookcase.* FRANK *sits with the latest letter at the table where* CECILY *has been sitting.*

HELENE *has risen with a leather-bound book in one hand and two large pages from the Clarendon Press with creases in them.*

HELENE Well!!! All I have to say to *you*, Frank Doel, is we live in depraved, destructive and degenerate times when a bookshop – a *bookshop* – starts tearing up beautiful old books to use as wrapping paper. I said to Cardinal Newman when he stepped out of his wrapping: Would you believe a thing like that, John Henry? And he said he wouldn't. You tore that book up in the middle of a major battle and I don't even know *which war it was!*

FRANK *looks up in delight.* HELENE *puts down the wrapping and moves to her sofa with the Newman.*

The Newman arrived almost a week ago and I am just beginning to recover. I keep it on the table with me all day. Every now and then I stop typing and reach over and touch it. Not because it's a first edition; I just never saw a book so beautiful... I feel vaguely guilty about owning it.

FRANK *has been glowing all through this. Suddenly he senses* MEGAN *watching him. He turns to look back at her with a shy smile. Then she goes on reading.*

HELENE *picks up the Newman and puts it on her shelves.*

All that gleaming leather and gold belongs in the library of an English country home; it wants to be read by the fire in a gentleman's leather easy chair – not in a one-room hovel in a broken-down brownstone front.

MEGAN *moves to table centre and sits. She has found the reference for which she was looking. She is joined by* CECILY.

HELENE *rises and returns to her desk and starts writing.*

I want the Q anthology.

Picks up the wrapping.

Why don't you wrap it in pages LCXII AND LCXIII so I can at least find out who won the battle and what war it was?

FRANK *laughs silently.*

P.S. Have you got Sam Pepys's *Diary* over there? I need him for long winter nights!

She exits.

FRANK *puts his spectacles in his pocket and the letter in his inside pocket.* **MEGAN** *rings the bell and* **BILL** *enters.*

FRANK Dear Miss Hanff: I am sorry for the delay in answering your letter but I have been out of town for a week or so and am now busy trying to catch up on my correspondence.

MEGAN *hands a pile of books to* **BILL** *and makes an invoice.* **CECILY** *appears upstage left, and climbs the stepladder.*

Please don't worry about us using old books such as Clarendon's *Rebellion* for wrapping. In this particular case there were just two odd volumes with the covers detached, and nobody in their right senses would have given us a shilling for them.

HELENE *looks up in amazement at this. She obviously thinks they are out of their minds. She shrugs and goes on writing.*

About the Sir Roger de Coverley *Papers...*

He moves towards a pile of books on the floor where he will find the de Coverley.

we happen to have in stock a volume of eighteenth-century essays, which includes a good selection of them as well as essays by Chesterfield and Goldsmith... It is edited by Austin Dobson...

He checks this and hands the book to MEGAN, *who reaches out to take it, but he withdraws it to look at it again.*

and is quite a nice edition, and as it is only one dollar fifteen we are sending it off to you by book post.

He now hands it to MEGAN *and crosses round the desk to the hat stand for his hat, coat and briefcase.*

The Quiller-Couch anthology, *The Pilgrim's Way*, is being sent to you in the same parcel. The balance due is...

He hesitates.

MEGAN *(prompts him:)* One dollar eighty-five.

FRANK *One* dollar eighty-five.

He hands the second book to MEGAN.

So your two dollars more than covered it. We haven't a copy of Pepys's *Diary* in stock at the moment but shall look out one for you.

He is now at the door.

It may interest you to know there are six of us in the shop, not including Mr Marks and Mr Cohen. With best wishes, F. Doel. For Marks and Company.

He exits.

MEGAN *takes the books to* BILL.

CECILY *comes down the stepladder and moves towards the crate.*

CECILY Helene, my dear. There are many ways of doing it but Mummy and I think this is the simplest for you to try.

*HELENE gets up, putting on an apron as she listens
to the recipe.*

Put a cup of flour, an egg, half a cup of milk and a good
shake of salt into a large bowl and beat all together until
it is the consistency of thick cream. Put it in the fridge for
several hours. It's best if you make it in the morning. When
you put your roast in the oven, put in an extra pan to heat.
Half an hour before your roast is done, pour a bit of the
roast grease into the baking pan, just enough to cover the
bottom will do. The pan must be *very hot*. Now pour the
pudding in and the roast and the pudding will be ready at
the same time.

*HELENE starts to go to her kitchen but is arrested by
the next line.*

I don't quite know how to describe it to someone who has
never seen it, but a good Yorkshire pudding will puff up
very high and brown and crisp, and when you cut into it
you will find that it is...hollow inside.

HELENE exits and CECILY breaks to behind desk.

The RAF is still keeping Doug in Norfolk and we are firmly
hoarding your Christmas tins until he comes home, but oh,
my dear, what a celebration we shall have when he does! I
do think you oughtn't to spend your money like that.

She snatches up her letter.

Must fly and post this if you're going to have it for Brian's
birthday dinner, do let me know if it's a success. Love, Cecily.

*False exit as HELENE re-enters, without her apron,
carrying a mug of coffee.*

HELENE Dear Cecily, Yorkshire pudding out of this world!

CECILY goes to share this latest letter with MEGAN.

We have nothing like it. I had to describe it to somebody as a high, curved, smooth, empty waffle!

HELENE *picks up the food catalogue and sits on her sofa.* **CECILY** *slowly drifts down to centre table and sits reading the letter. When it gets to the description of the parcels,* **MEGAN** *will join her, standing looking over her shoulder, also reading the letter.*

Please don't worry about what the food parcels cost.

I have such a time with the catalogue. I spread it out on the rug and debate the relative merits of parcel 105 (includes one dozen eggs and a tin of sweet biscuits) or parcel 217 B, two dozen eggs and no sweet biscuits). I hate the one dozen egg parcels. What is two eggs for anyone to take home? And no sweet biscuits? So it's a problem.

BILL *enters and puts mail on* **FRANK**'*s desk.* **MEGAN** *and* **CECILY** *invite him to share in* **HELENE**'*s latest letter.*

A producer who likes my plays – but not enough to produce them – just phoned. He's producing a TV series, do I want to write for television? "Two bills", he said carelessly, which turns out to mean 200 dollars. And me a forty-dollar-a-week script-reader! I go down to see him tomorrow, keep your fingers crossed... Best, Helene.

She types.

The three cross their fingers.

MEGAN *crosses to* **FRANK**'*s desk,* **CECILY** *to the chair at the table by the side of the desk, while* **BILL** *sits at centre table, behind a pile of books, writing his letter. Each, unknown to the other, is writing to* **HELENE**.

CECILY Helene, dear, your marvellous Easter parcels arrived safely and everyone is quite upset because Frank left the city on business for the firm the next morning and so hasn't written to thank you, and of course no one else quite dares to write to Frank's Miss Hanff. Love, Cecily.

She exits, picking up a pile of books.

HELENE *puts down* **CECILY**'s *letter and almost at once is picking up* **MEGAN**'s. **MEGAN** *is writing swiftly as she speaks, her voice low, looking round to check no one is watching.*

MEGAN Dear Miss Hanff: This is just to let you know that your Easter parcels to Marks and Company arrived safely a few days ago, but have not been acknowledged as Frank Doel is away from the office on business for the firm.

She looks around, then continues in an even quieter voice. She moves away from the desk, very confidential.

I did feel I must write and tell you how exceedingly grateful we all are for your kindness and generousity. We all hope that you will be able to come to England one of these days. We should do our best to make your trip a happy one.

She looks around.

Sincerely, Megan Wells.

She hurries out with her letter.

Immediately, as **BILL** *speaks,* **HELENE** *picks up the third letter.* **BILL** *looks round first before speaking.*

BILL *(rising)* Dear Miss Hanff: For nearly two years I have been working as a cataloguer at Marks and Company, and would like to thank you very much for my share-out in the parcels which you have been sending.

He moves to **FRANK**'s *desk, picking up mail.*

I live with my great-aunt who is seventy-five, and I think that if you had seen the look of delight on her face when I brought home the meat and the tin of tongue, you would have realised just how grateful we are.

He moves downstage to pick up two books on the crate.

It's certainly good to know that someone so many miles away can be so kind and generous to people they haven't even seen...

He begins to exit.

and I think that everyone in the firm feels the same. Sincerely, Bill Humphries.

He exits swiftly, and simultaneously FRANK *enters the shop swiftly, with his hat, briefcase and umbrella. With his hand on the door he speaks at once.*

FRANK Dear Miss Hanff: I expect you are getting a bit worried that we have not written to thank you for your parcels – thinking that we are an ungrateful lot.

HELENE *raises the four letters with amusement.*

The truth is that I have been chasing around the country...

He is closing the shop door, hanging up his hat and umbrella and placing his briefcase on the table.

in and out of various stately homes of England, trying to buy a few books to fill up our sadly depleted stocks. My wife was starting to call me the lodger who just went home for bed and breakfast, but of course when I arrived home with a nice piece of M-E-A-T, to say nothing of dried eggs and ham, then she thought I was a fine fellow and all was forgiven. I must say, it is a long time since we saw so much meat all in one piece.

He is now downstage centre.

We should like to express our appreciation in some way or other, so we are sending you by book post today...

*He is removing from his jacket pocket a small book.
Simultaneously* HELENE *picks up an identical book.*

.a little book, which I hope you will like.

*Simultaneously they are moving towards each other, each
holding a book. Facing front, they are now very close.*

I remember you asked me for a volume of Elizabethan
love poems some time ago – well, this is the nearest I can
get to it.

HELENE *removes from her copy a small card, which
she reads.*

HELENE To Helene Hanff...

FRANK With best wishes and grateful thanks for many kindnesses
from...

He pauses. He would like to send it from himself.

all at 84 Charing Cross Road, London, April 1951.

HELENE Thank you for the beautiful book. I've never owned
a book before with pages edged all round in gold. Would
you believe it arrived on my birthday!

She opens it and begins to read a Shakespeare sonnet.

Let me not to the marriage of true minds...

FRANK Admit impediments...

There are tears in HELENE's *eyes but she holds them
back. They are quite close.*

HELENE Love is not loved which alteration finds...

FRANK Or bends with the remover to remove...

HELENE Oh, no, it is an ever-fixed mark...

FRANK That looks on tempests and is never shaken.

HELENE *looks again at the card.*

HELENE I wish you hadn't been so over-courteous about putting the inscription on a card instead of on the flyleaf. It's the bookseller coming out in all of you, you were afraid you'd decrease its value. You would have increased it for the present owner. And possibly for the future owner.

And why didn't you sign your names?

FRANK *slips the book in his pocket and turns to exit. He is halfway out when he is arrested by the next words and turns round.*

I expect Frank wouldn't let you, he probably doesn't want me writing love letters to anybody but him!

FRANK, *caught out, shyly runs his finger round the inside of his collar, and grins coyly.*

Swift exit.

HELENE *is alone. Light change, as though a storm is pending, sky darkening.* **HELENE** *moves to her desk and lights a cigarette.*

I send you greetings from America – faithless friend that she is, pouring millions into rebuilding Japan and Germany while letting England starve. Some day, God willing, I'll get over there and apologise personally for my country's sins (and by the time I come home, my country will certainly have to apologise for mine!). Thank you again for the beautiful book, I shall try very hard not to get gin and ashes all over it. It's really too fine for the likes of me!

She moves upstage and slowly puts on her jacket.

Music is now heard: the opening bars of Vaughan Williams' "FANTASIA ON A THEME BY THOMAS TALLIS".

We now see **MAXINE,** *elegantly dressed – large picture-frame hat – coming down the street. She pauses briefly to browse outside. She opens the door, pauses as she* *takes in the shop, moves centre. Music out before she speaks. The shop is full of shadows. As she begins to speak, so* **HELENE** *turns front, leans against her desk, listening intently.*

MAXINE Dear heart, it is the loveliest old shop straight out of Dickens, you would go absolutely out of your mind about it. There are stalls outside, and I stopped and leafed through a few things – just to establish myself as a browser, before wandering in.

It's dim inside – you smell the shop before you see it; it's a lovely smell. I can't articulate it easily but it combines must and dust and age, and walls of wood and floors of wood.

She moves upstage towards **MR MARTIN***'s table.*

Towards the back of the shop there's a desk with a work lamp on it. A man was sitting there. He was about sixty, with a Hogarth nose. He looked up and said "Good afternoon" in a North Country accent, and I said I just wanted to browse and he said please do.

The shelves go on for ever. They go up to the ceiling. They are very old and kind of grey, like old oak that has absorbed so much dust over the years they no longer are their true colour.

There's a print section with Cruikshank and Rackham and Spy and all those old wonderful English caricaturists and illustrators that I'm not smart enough to know a lot about, and there are some lovely, old illustrated magazines.

She sits on a hamper downstage with one of the magazines.

I stayed for about half an hour, hoping your Frank or one of the girls would turn up, but it was one-ish when I went in. I gather they were all out to lunch, and I couldn't stay any longer.

She makes up her mind to buy one for **HELENE**.

As you will see, the notices for our play were not sensational, but we're told they're good enough to assure us a few months run, so – yesterday – I went apartment-hunting and found a nice little "bed-sitter" in Knightsbridge! I don't have the address here, I'll send it or...you can call my mother.

She rises, looking for somewhere to put her coins, crosses to FRANK*'s desk and rests her handbag on it. She puts coins in the duck's back, which we now realise is a money box.*

We have no food problems, we eat in restaurants and hotels. The best places like Claridge's get all the roast beef and chops they want. The prices are astronomical but the exchange rate is so good we can afford it. Of course, if I were English I would loathe us, instead of which they are absolutely wonderful to us; we're invited to everybody's home and everybody's club. The only thing we can't get is sugar or sweets in any form, for which I personally thank God. I intend to lose pounds over here.

HELENE *laughs.*

Do you remember when we first met in the ladies' room at the Morosco Theatre and I couldn't get my falsies to stay put. And you said, "You don't need falsies, you've got a perfect figure." And I said, "I wouldn't have got the part if they had known I was flat chested!"

Well, I have found the most perfect bra with built-in falsies and where do you think I got it? No, not at Harrods, but at a tiny little shop in Kensington called Il Morocco! How about that? What you say I bring back some for you? I tell you what, when we next walk down Broadway they aren't going to recognise us!

Write me. Love, Maxine.

HELENE   Maxine, bless your golden heart, what a peachy description, you write better than I do.

She moves behind her desk to put out her cigarette.

I don't like to sound bitter but I would like to know what *you* ever did that the good Lord lets *you* browse around my bookshop while I'm stuck on Ninety-Fifth Street, writing the TV *Adventures of Ellery Queen.*

MAXINE *laughs.* **HELENE** *stubs out her cigarette.*

Did I tell you we're not allowed to use a lip-stained cigarette for a clue?

She holds up her stub. Then picks up ashtray and empties it in bin.

We're sponsored by the Bayuk Cigar Company and we're not allowed to mention the word cigarette. We can have ashtrays on the set but they can't have any cigarette butts in them. They can't have cigar butts either, they're not pretty.

She returns the empty ashtray to the desk.

All an ashtray can have in it is a wrapped, unsmoked Bayuk cigar.

The music of Eric Coates' "LONDON SUITE - KNIGHTSBRIDGE", is heard. Helene moves front, hands in pockets.

Write me about London, the Tube, the Inns of Court, Mayfair, the corner where the Globe Theatre stood, anything, I'm not fussy.

MAXINE *moves to the door of the shop and turns on the word "Knightsbridge".* Write me about Knightsbridge, it sounds green and gracious in Eric Coates's "London Suite".

MAXINE *blows a kiss. She slowly exits, taking a last lingering look at the shop. She closes door and goes down the street.*

Music still playing, HELENE *returns to work, finds the Pepys's* Diary *that has just arrived, flicks through it, and suddenly shuts the book with a loud bang.*

Mr Doel! *What kind of a Pepys's* Diary *do you call this?* This is not Pepys' *Diary,* this is some busybody editor's miserable collection of *excerpts* from Pepys's *Diary* may he rot. I could just spit!

FRANK *enters in a hurry, agitated, holding* HELENE's *letter, which has two dollars clipped to it, underneath it. He grabs his spectacles from the desk and comes down front, reading.*

Where is January 12th 1688, where his wife chased him out of bed and around the bedroom with a red-hot poker?

FRANK Mrs Farr!

CECILY *hurries on.* FRANK *glares at her – she looks guiltily.*

HELENE Where is Sir William Penn's son that was giving everybody so much trouble with his Quaker notions? *One* mention does he get in this whole pseudo-book. And me, from Philadelphia!

She moves upstage.

I enclose two limp singles.

FRANK *looks, finds them, detaches them and hands them at arm's length to* CECILY, *as though she were responsible.*

I will make do with this thing until you find me a real Pepys. *Then* I will tear up this ersatz book, page by page, and *wrap things in it!*

FRANK *sinks onto crate centre stage.*

Fresh eggs or powdered for Christmas?

FRANK, surprised by her sudden change of tone, looks round at CECILY, who is upstage by the work table, where she is making out an invoice. She looks at him, laughs, and exits.

I know the powdered last longer but "fresh eggs flown from Denmark" have to taste better. You want to take a vote on it?

FRANK speaks very swiftly, as if to make amends. He is in a manic state of guilt and quite distraught. HELENE listens intently to see what excuses he will come out with.

FRANK   Dear Miss Hanff, First of all let me apologise for the Samuel Pepys's *Diary*. I was honestly under the impression that it was the complete Braybrooke edition and I can understand how you must have felt when you found your favourite passages missing. I promise to look at the next reasonably priced copy that comes along and if it contains the passages you mention in your letter I will send it along.

HELENE exits here.

BILL now enters with two crates of books on a trolley, followed by CECILY with an armful of books, followed by MEGAN with a checklist.

MR MARTIN, in a muffler, hat and gloves, enters from the street and surveys the activity with raised eyebrows. They are all in a panic. They have never seen FRANK like this before.

I am glad to say, I am very glad to say, I have managed to dig out a few books for you from a private library that we have just bought.

MEGAN and CECILY are now downstage, sorting books.

BILL is still unloading. As FRANK approaches CECILY hands him the Leigh Hunt.

There is a Leigh Hunt *(He holds it up in triumph.)* – which includes most of the essays you like.

He is now between the two girls.

There is also a Vulgate New Testament *(He holds this up in triumph.)* – which I hope will be – okay!

The girls look at him in amazement. Could he have been drinking?

He now charges across to stage left in search of more books.

I have also included a dictionary to the Vulgate...

But he cannot find it. **MEGAN** *looks to see if it is in one of the crates.* **BILL**, *who has joined* **CECILY** *in sorting books, hands the dictionary to* **FRANK**...

which you might find useful. There is also a volume of twentieth-century English essays, though it contains only one by Hilaire Belloc – and nothing to do with bathrooms.

MEGAN *does a double take at this non sequitur, then moves upstage to desk area.* **FRANK** *moves in front of his desk, stage left.*

Enclosed is our invoice for seventeen shillings and sixpence or approximately...

In his excitement and guilt he still can't think clearly. **MEGAN**, *making out the invoice, looks up, eyebrows raised, and prompts him.*

MEGAN Two dollars fifty!

FRANK Two dollars fifty! All that is due to us on the books, as you had a credit balance with us of nearly two dollars.

FRANK *is now behind his desk, clutching the books. He looks across at the others, almost absent-mindedly. As he speaks about them, they look up.*

About the eggs...I have talked to the rest of the inmates here, and we all seem to think that the fresh ones would be nicer...as you say, they will not last as long, but they will taste...ah...much, ah, much...

MEGAN Better!

They all nod in agreement.

FRANK Yes, better... We are all hoping for better things after the General Election. If Churchill and Company get in, as I think and hope they will, it will cheer everyone up immensely.

He begins to exit upstairs.

With best wishes, Yours sincerely, Frank Doel.

He is hurrying off but the others arrest him.

OTHERS *(aghast)* For Marks and Company!

FRANK *stops.*

FRANK For Marks and Company!

He exits

The OTHERS *also exit,* BILL *last with the trolley.*

HELENE *enters, holding two books.*

HELENE Dear Speed! You dizzy me, rushing Leigh Hunt and the Vulgate over here whizzbang like that. You probably don't realise it but it's hardly more than two years since I ordered them. You keep going at this rate, you're gonna give yourself a heart attack.

Light changes to winter.

That's mean. You just go to so much trouble for me and I never even thank you. I just needle you, it's mean. I really am grateful for all the pains you take for me.

She has put the two books down on the sofa and now
goes back to her desk to find money and an envelope.
Her mug of coffee is standing on top of the dollars.

I enclose three dollars. Sorry about the top one. I spilled
coffee on it and it wouldn't sponge off, but I think it's still
good. You can still read it.

We hear the beginning of "UNTO US A CHILD IS BORN"
from Handel's "MESSIAH".

Do you carry hardcover scores by any chance? Like Bach's
St Matthew's Passion and Handel's *Messiah*? I could
probably get them here at Schirmer's but they're fifty cold
blocks from where I live so I thought I'd ask you first.

The envelope is now sealed and she drops it into her 'box'.
She comes round to the side of her desk and, stooping,
picks up a bottle of gin from the floor and a glass. She
puts the glass on the desk and unscrews the bottle.

Congratulations on Churchill and Company. I hope he
loosens up your rations a little. (*pours drink, lifts glass*)
Is your name Welsh?

She exits.

Music swells. From upstage centre a loud burst of
squeakers. FRANK *enters unsteadily, wearing a paper*
hat, carrying a glass of wine. He goes to his desk.

FRANK Dear Miss Hanff! You will be glad to know that the two
boxes of eggs and the tins of tongue have all arrived safely
and once again we all wish to thank you most sincerely for
your extreme generosity.

There is a loud burst of squeakers. Enter MEGAN, BILL
and CECILY, *all in paper party hats.* BILL *also wears a*
false nose and carries a sprig of mistletoe. They push
CECILY, *who kisses* FRANK *on the cheek. They laugh*
and blow squeakers again. It is the middle of the office

Christmas party. **FRANK**, *realising he has got lipstick on his cheek, puts down his glass on the table at the side of his desk and gets out his handkerchief to wipe off the lipstick. The* **OTHERS**, *watching from upstage, blow their squeakers again. He turns, waving them off, and they go out.*

Mr Martin, one of the older members of our staff, has been on the sick list for some time and we therefore let him have the—

Here, in picking up his glass, he accidentally knocks two small books onto the floor. He looks round guiltily.

Oh, dear! *(picks them up)* The lion's share of the eggs, one whole boxful in fact, and of course he was delighted to get them.

The tins of tongue look very inviting and will be a welcome addition to our larders, and in my case will be put on one side for a special occasion.

The three now enter with a large wrapped box, and **MEGAN** *has labels to stick on it.*

Oh, yes! We are sending you a little gift for Christmas.

Music out.

It is linen and we hope that you will not have to pay any duty on it. We will mark it...

He pauses, at a loss. **MEGAN** *prompts him.*

MEGAN Christmas gift!

FRANK Christmas gift! And keep our fingers crossed.

BILL *starts to exit to post the parcel.*

Anyway, we hope you will like it and accept it with our sincere best wishes for Christmas...

He pauses.

BILL *turns,* **MEGAN** *and* **CECILY** *accompany him:*

OTHERS And the coming year!

FRANK And the coming year. Yes!

FRANK *lurches to behind his desk and leans over it, still holding his glass.*

(belligerently) My name is certainly not of Welsh origin. As it is pronounced to rhyme with the French word "Noel" ...

MEGAN *and* **CECILY** *start to sing* **"THE FIRST NOEL",** *quietly sending him up.* **FRANK** *looks up, amused.*

I think there may be a possibility that it originated in France!

BILL *is now back and joins in the singing, as does* **FRANK,** *conducting them. At the end of the fourth line they hum, and over this* **HELENE** *re-enters with a Christmas card in one hand and the box, minus wrapping, in the other.*

HELENE *(reading from card)* Christmas greetings and all good wishes for the New Year from George Martin...

BILL Bill Humphries

MEGAN Megan Wells

CECILY Cecily Farr

FRANK Frank Doel

HELENE J. Pemberton?

In the shop they sing a chorus of **"THE FIRST NOEL".** **FRANK** *collects the paper hats and exits with* **BILL.**

MEGAN *sits upstage by* **MR MARTIN**'s *desk, and* **CECILY** *at the centre table.* **HELENE** *lifts the tablecloth out of the box.*

Maxine! Wait till you see what the shop sent me for Christmas! It's an Irish linen tablecloth, the colour of thick cream, hand-embroidered in an old-fashioned pattern of leaves and flowers, every flower worked in a different colour, and shaded from very pale to very deep. You never saw anything like it. My junk-shop drop-leaf table certainly never saw anything like it. I get this urge...

She is pouring out gin and pours it like tea from a silver tea pot.

to shake out my flowing Victorian sleeve and lift a graceful arm to pour tea from an imaginary Georgian teapot.

She exits with tablecloth, box and glass.

FRANK *enters from back of shop, crossing to his desk.*

FRANK 17th January, 1952

Dear Miss Hanff, First of all we are so glad that you liked the cloth. It gave us a lot of pleasure to send it and it was one little way of thanking you for all your kind gifts over the last few years. You may be interested to know that it was embroidered, quite recently, by an old lady of over eighty, who lives in the flat – ah, apartment! next door to me. She lives all by herself and does quite a lot of needlework as a hobby. She does not often part with any of her work, but my wife managed to persuade her to sell this cloth, and I think she also made her a present of some of the dried egg you sent us, which helped a lot.

He has collected his hat, briefcase and umbrella.

If you must wash your Bible...we should advise ordinary soap and water. Put a teaspoon of soda in a pint of warm water...and use a soapy sponge. I think you will find this removes the dirt...and you can then polish it with a little lanolin!

He exits by shop door.

HELENE *lifts two or three TV scripts.*

HELENE Maxine! The *Ellery Queen* series raised me to 250 dollars a script. If it keeps up till June I may get to England and browse around my bookshop myself. If I have the nerve.

I write them the most outrageous letters from a safe 3000 miles away. I'll probably walk in there one day and walk right out again without telling them who I am.

She moves downstage.

I fail to see why you did not understand that grocery man in Knightsbridge. He did not call it "ground ground nuts". He called it "ground ground-nuts" which is the only sensible thing to call it. Peanuts grow in the ground and are therefore ground-nuts, and after you have taken them out of the ground you grind them up and you have ground ground-nuts, which is a much more accurate name than peanut butter. You just don't understand English. Kisses. H. Hanff, girl etymologist.

She turns, then swings back.

P.S. I have just talked to your mother. She says you don't think the show in London will run another month, and she says you took two dozen pairs of nylons over there, so do me a favour. As soon as the closing notice goes up, take three pairs of nylons around to the bookshop for me, give them to Frank Doel, tell him they're for the two girls and Nora, his wife. I'll reimburse you for them.

On the words "closing notice" **CECILY** *checks her watch, rises, goes to the shop door, turns the "OPEN" sign round to "CLOSED" and locks the door. She goes over to* **MEGAN** *– it's time to go to the funeral. Both exit upstage right.*

Frank Doel, you sloth! I could rot over here before you send me anything to read. You may add Walton's *Lives* to the list of books you aren't sending me. You can't even get Walton's *Lives* from a library here. You can look at it. They have one down at the 42nd branch. But not to take *home*! The lady said to me, shocked. *"Read it here"*. Just sit down in Room 315 and read the whole book without a cup of coffee, a cigarette or air.

Sound of church bells.

From the street a procession appears. FRANK *opens the door and* BILL *appears first, with a black mourning band around his arm.* MEGAN *follows with a black hat, and* CECILY *with a black scarf over her head.* CECILY *reverses the sign to "OPEN".* FRANK *carries, as usual, his hat, briefcase and umbrella. He, too, has a black mourning band on his arm.* BILL *exits.* CECILY *and* MEGAN *slowly remove headgear, look at* FRANK *and then* CECILY *exits to make coffee for them.*

What do you do with yourself all day? Sit in the back of the store and read? Why don't you try selling books to somebody? And why am I still Miss Hanff to you? I'm Helene to my friends.

P.S. Tell the girls and Nora, if all goes well they're getting nylons for Lent.

FRANK *is now behind his desk.*

FRANK Dear Helene!

HELENE *looks up at this.* At last! *Then continues with her work.*

I quite agree it is time we dropped the "Miss" when writing to you. I am not really so stand-offish, as you may have been led to believe, but as copies of the letters I have written to you go into the office files, the formal address seemed more appropriate. But as this letter has nothing to do with books, there will be no copy.

We are quite at a loss to know how you managed the nylons, which appeared this noon as if by magic. All I can tell you is that when I came back from lunch they were on my desk with a note reading "From Helene Hanff".

Enter CECILY *with the coffee on a tray, three cups. She puts the tray down on the centre table and takes her own cup and saucer, while* MEGAN *carries the sugar bowl and a spoon.*

No one seems to know how or when they arrived.

He looks across at the girls.

The girls are very thrilled and I believe they are planning to write to you themselves.

MEGAN *hands him his cup and puts a spoonful of sugar in it for him.*

Pause.

CECILY *goes to sit at head of centre table with her coffee.*

I am sorry to say that our friend Mr George Martin, who has been ill for some time, has passed away in hospital last week. He was with the firm a great number of years, so what with his loss and the King dying so suddenly as well, we are rather a mournful crowd at present.

He moves away with his cup, coming down front of the desk. MEGAN *gives* CECILY *a look and stands, sipping her coffee.*

I don't see how we can ever repay you for your many kind gifts. All I can say is, if ever you decide to make the trip to England, there will be a bed for you at 37 Oakfield Court for as long as you care to stay. With all good wishes, Frank.

HELENE Oh, my! *(pause)* I do bless you for this Walton's *Lives.* It's incredible that a book published in 1840 can be in such perfect condition more than a hundred years later. Such beautiful, mellow, rough-cut pages they are.

BILL appears and signals to CECILY, *who exits.* MEGAN *sits at the work table, sipping coffee.* FRANK *still stands downstage, holding his cup and saucer.* HELENE *moves downstage.*

I do feel for poor William T. Gordon, who wrote his name in it in 1841.

What a crummy lot of descendents he must have – to sell it to you casually, for nothing. Boy, I'd like to have run barefoot through their library before they sold it. Fascinating book to read.

Did you know John Donne eloped with the boss's highborn daughter and landed in the Tower for it and starved and starved and then got religion, my word!

She puts down the book. FRANK *turns and puts his cup on the desk, sees* MEGAN *watching, and smiles. She resumes working. He moves to the hat stand and quietly removes his arm band.* HELENE *rises, crosses to the sofa for her handbag and takes out money.*

Now listen – I'm enclosing a five-dollar bill. That Walton's *Lives* makes me very dissatisfied with my *Angler*, which I bought before I met you. So use the extra two dollars fifty for a nice English *Angler*, please.

She drops letter into the 'box' and resumes work.

You better watch out.

FRANK *is now back at his desk.*

I'm coming over in '53 if *Ellery* is renewed.

FRANK *looks up and across at* MEGAN. *They are excited.* MEGAN *now exits to tell* CECILY *and* BILL.

I'm gonna climb up that Victorian book ladder and disturb the dust and everybody's decorum. Or didn't I ever tell you I write arty murders for *Ellery Queen* on television? All my scripts have artistic backgrounds: ballet, concert hall, opera; and all the suspects and the corpses are cultured. Maybe I'll write one about the rare-book business in your honour – you want to be the murderer or the corpse?

FRANK *lifts his file with a flourish. Opens desk and deposits it inside.*

FRANK Dear Helene, You see, I don't care about the files any more!

BILL *enters with another trolley full of books, followed by* MEGAN *and* CECILY *with armfuls of books.* CECILY *goes downstage right,* MEGAN *to centre table, and* BILL *unpacks books at the table to the side of* FRANK's *desk.*

You will be pleased to know we have just purchased a private library which includes a very nice copy of Walton's *Compleat Angler*, and will be sending it to you today.

He is putting away his files, then picks up his briefcase and hat – a Panama this time – and umbrella from the hat stand.

Your *Ellery Queen* scripts sound rather fun. I wish we could have a chance of seeing some of them on our TV over here – it wants livening up a bit. Our TV, I mean, not your script!

He moves to centre stage, holding his Panama hat.

BILL *has just discovered an unusual first edition and draws* FRANK's *attention to it. He will move on from* BILL *to* MEGAN *and down to* CECILY, *arriving by the end of* HELENE's *speech.*

HELENE Dear Frank, The woodcuts in Walton's *Angler* alone are worth ten times the price of the book. What a peculiar world we live in when so beautiful a thing can be owned for life or for the price of a ticket to a Broadway movie. But, if your books cost what they're worth, I couldn't afford them.

Regards to Nora and the wage slaves.

FRANK Dear Helene, Thirty volumes of Loeb's Classics have come in, but, alas, no Horace, no Sappho, no Catullus.

I am taking a couple of weeks' holiday...

He puts on his Panama hat at a jaunty angle and walks across front of stage. The **OTHERS** *listen.*

but as I have just bought a car, we are completely broke, so we'll have to take things easy. Nora has a sister who lives by the sea so we are hoping she will take pity on us and invite us to stay with her.

It is my first car, so we are all very thrilled with it – even though it is an old 1939 model. So long as it gets us to places without breaking down too often we shall be quite happy. With all good wishes, Frank.

Umbrella at an angle, like a rifle, he strides off. The **OTHERS** *resume work.*

HELENE *looks up.*

HELENE Hey, Frankie! How about if I came over next year in time for the Coronation?

She starts typing.

The **OTHERS** *all react to this.*

We hear the honk of **FRANK**'s *car and the starting noises.*

As a joke, **BILL,** *picking up his ukelele, starts to sing "MY OLD MAN SAYS FOLLOW THE VAN!"* **MEGAN** *and* **CECILY** *pick this up, and cross to the window, arms full of books, to watch* **FRANK** *drive off.*

Hey, Frankie, how about if I come over in time for the Coronation?

She starts singing the chorus of "COMING OVER":

OVER THERE, OVER THERE, THE YANKS ARE COMING.

The rest of the staff join in, adapting the words to

SHE'S COMING OVER...

And bringing armfuls of books downstage to the long bench... The singing ends, with **HELENE** *solo on the final line*

AND WE WONT COME BACK TILL IT'S OVER THERE

Her hand up in the air, and the staff all looking out front in excited expectation.

Curtain.

ACT II

Inside the shop FRANK, *in a linen jacket, is on the phone to a customer. The wooden crate has been moved from centre stage to stage left.*

The curtain rises to the music of "ON THE TOWN".

Outside, bunting is hung from the shop windows in readiness for the coronation. BILL *now wears a tweed jacket.*

FRANK A Bradenham edition of *Disraeli*? I sold one last month. Twelve volumes, black cloth.

I suppose you want one with the dust wrappers? I think your best bet would be Foyles. As you come out of the lift there on the second floor, turn left, and it's in the third bay on the right – somewhere around shoulder height. The first volume's got an ugly bookplate in it, otherwise there's nothing wrong with it, and they want £125 as far as I can remember. *(pause)* Not at all. Good luck!

He picks up the small bell and MEGAN *takes the phone from him back into the inner office.*

HELENE *enters, singing from "ON THE TOWN", carrying a cardboard box. She is spring-cleaning her books.*

HELENE Hey, Frankie! Guess who came while you were away on vacation? Sam Pepys!

Music out. She pauses to touch the three slim volumes on her desk.

Those in the shop disperse to sorting and arranging books.

Please thank whoever mailed him. He came a week ago. He stepped right out of the pages of some tabloid, three honest navy-blue volumes of him. I read the tabloid over lunch and started Sam after dinner.

HELENE *is stuffing books into the box. She checks titles and occasionally decides not to throw one out.*

He says to tell you he's overjoyed to be here; he was previously owned by a slob who never even bothered to cut the pages. I'm wrecking them; it's the thinnest onion paper I ever saw. But heavier paper would have taken up six or seven volumes and I have very few books left to throw out.

BILL *by now is working at table upstage. He has replaced* **MR MARTIN.** **CECILY** *and* **MEGAN** *exit.*

FRANK *finishes arranging the display on table centre stage and exits upstage left on the next line.*

I house-clean my books every spring and throw out those I'm never going to read again, like I throw out clothes I'm never going to wear again.

My friends are peculiar about books. They read all the bestsellers. They go through them as fast as possible. I think they skip a lot. And they NEVER read anything a second time, so they don't remember a word of it a year later. But they're profoundly shocked to see me drop a book in the wastepaper basket or give it away. The way they look at it, you buy a book, you read it, you put it on the shelf, you never open it again for the rest of your life, but *you don't throw it out! Not if it has a hard cover on it!* Why not? I personally can't think of anything less sacrosanct than a bad book.

During the last sentence **HELENE** *has dumped the box of books in her hall way and is seated back at her desk.* **FRANK** *has entered from upstage and sits on the library*

ladder reading a book. MEGAN *enters a moment later.*
BILL *exits up the stairs.*

Trust you and Nora had a fine holiday. Mine was spent in
Central Park. I had a month's vacation from Joey, my dear
little dentist; he went on his honeymoon. I financed it!
Did I tell you he told me last spring I had to have all my
teeth capped or all my teeth out? I decided to have them
capped as I have got used to having teeth. The cost is simply
astronomical. So Elizabeth will have to ascend the throne
without me: teeth are all I am going to see crowned for
the next couple of years. I do not intend to stop buying
books, however...

P.S. I plan to crawl out of bed before dawn on Coronation
Day to attend the ceremony by radio. *(She takes out from
her desk drawer a small Union Jack flag, which she sticks
in a vase.)* Will be thinking of you all. Cheers!

Major light change.

*We hear an excerpt from the radio broadcast of the
coronation.* HELENE, *in a dressing gown, enters, listening
to it on her radio.*

*We hear part of the BBC recording of the coronation of
Queen Elizabeth II, the section where John Snagge speaks
of the Queen Mother waiting to see her daughter present
herself to her people waiting outside the west door of
Westminster Abbey, followed by the fanfare, and then
the whole congregation joining in singing the national
anthem.* HELENE *starts to sing along with this.*

FRANK *(seated high up on the stepladder)*

June 11th 1953.

Dear Helene, Just a note to let you know that your parcel
arrived safely on June 1st, just in time for our Coronation
celebrations. We had a number of friends at home to watch
TV on the day, and so the ham was most welcome to provide

them with something to eat. It was delicious. And we all drank to your health as well as the Queen's.

BILL *and* MEGAN *are seen outside the shop.* BILL *in his waistcoat, with a small stepladder. Slowly they begin to take down the decorations.*

It was most kind of you to spend your hard-earned money on us like this, and the rest of the staff join me in saying – *thanks a lot*!

He says this with a broad American accent – he turns and sees CECILY *observing him. She exits.*

HELENE Frankie, you'll *die* when I tell you. Now then. *Ellery Queen* went off the air and I was shuffling around piling up dentist's bills and feeling pale, when I was invited to write an outline for a TV show which dramatises incidents from the lives of famous people. So I rushed home and did an outline of an incident from-the-life-of-a-famous-person and sent it in and they bought it and I wrote the script and they liked it and they're gonna give me more work in the Fall. And whaddya think I dramatised? John Donne eloping with the boss's daughter, out of Walton's *Lives*.

FRANK *looks up at this.*

Nobody who watches television has the slightest idea who John Donne was – but thanks to Hemingway *everybody* knows "No man is an island". All I had to do was work that in and it was sold!

FRANK *shakes his head with amusement, collects his briefcase, umbrella and hat, and goes outside, closing the shop door. We can see him outside talking with* BILL *and* MEGAN *about a new window display, and then leaving.*

So that's how John Donne made the *Hallmark Hall of Fame* and paid for all the books you ever sent me and five teeth!

CECILY enters with a small round suitcase, and wool sweater, which she places on a downstage chair. She leaves a note on FRANK's desk.

CECILY Helene, dear, I'm dashing this off to say you must send nothing at all to the shop for Christmas. Everything is now off rations and even nylons are available in all the better shops. Please save your money, as the most important thing after your dentist is your trip to England. Only don't come in '54 as I shall be in Iraq with Doug, where he is now stationed. Come in '55, when we shall be back and you can stay with us.

She is putting on the wool jacket.

Doug writes that our call may come at any moment, as we are next in line for married quarters. The children and I are hoping to join him before Christmas. He is well and happy on Bahrain Island in the middle of the Persian Gulf (if you've got an atlas), but will return to the RAF base at Habbaniya in Iraq when our quarters are available and we will join him there, all being well.

She picks up the case. MEGAN and BILL are now entering the shop.

Write again soon. Best wishes...

She shakes BILL by the hand.

and love...

She kisses MEGAN, who breaks away to hide her tears. CECILY moves to the door of the shop.

Cecily.

MEGAN and BILL wave as she goes. BILL goes to desk up centre, and MEGAN exits to put away the bunting, then returns to sit at table centre stage.

HELENE *(rising with the Marks & Co catalogue)* Do you mean to sit there and tell me you've been publishing these mammoth catalogues all these years and this is the first time you ever bothered to send me one? Thou varlet!

I don't remember which Restoration playwright it was who called everyone a varlet! But I've always wanted to use it in a sentence! As it happens, the only thing which *might* interest me is the Catullus, it's not the Loeb Classics but it sounds like it'll do. If you still have it, mail it and I'll send you the six shillings twopence as soon as you translate it – Kay and Brian moved to the suburbs and left me without a translator.

Sound of New York church bells. From the sofa she picks up the New York Times.

I shall be obliged if you will send Nora and the girls to church every Sunday for the next month to pray for the continued health and strength of the Messrs Gilliam, Reese, Snider, Campanella, Robinson, Hodges, Furillo, Podres, Newcombe, and Labine, collectively known as the Brooklyn Dodgers. If they lose this World Series I shall do myself in and then where will you be?

She throws the paper back on the sofa, looks at her watch, sees the time and realises she's going to be late for a script conference. She shuffles the scripts into a briefcase, and winds a scarf round her neck.

Have you got de Tocqueville's *Journey to America*? Somebody borrowed mine and never gave it back. Why is it that people who wouldn't dream of stealing anything else think it's perfectly all right to steal books? Regards to Megan...

MEGAN *looks up.*

If she's still there. And what's become of Cecily, is she back from Iraq?

Sound of siren. She exits.

Wintry lighting. FRANK *in overcoat enters from the street. He wheezes and moves with difficulty. He has been ill and come back to work sooner than he should have.* BILL *and* MEGAN *register his arrival, and* MEGAN *flashes a silent signal, "go and get him a hot drink."*

FRANK December 13th 1955.

Dear Helene, I feel very guilty about not writing to you before this, but you can put it down to a dose of flu which kept me away from the shop for a couple of weeks.

MEGAN *takes his umbrella and puts his briefcase on the table.*

About the Catullus, I am sending you an edition which contains the Latin text with a verse translation by Sir Richard Burton, and also a prose translation by Leonard Smithers...

He is removing his gloves, stuffing them into pockets of his coat, then removes his overcoat, helped by MEGAN *who goes to hang it up. He rubs his hands together and goes to his desk, perching on a high stool.*

printed in large type and all for three dollars seventy-eight. We have no edition of de Tocqueville but will keep looking for one for you.

MEGAN *is now stage right of him.*

Megan is still here but planning to go to South Africa to live; we are all trying to talk her out of it.

MEGAN, *mock indignant, whips his hat off his head and crosses to the hat stand.*

Cecily has left and gone out to the Middle East to join her husband, although he was only to be gone a year...

BILL *appears with a hot drink, which* MEGAN *takes from him and brings down to* FRANK *who is at work at his desk.* MEGAN *waits, holding the drink.*

I shall be only too pleased to root for the Brooklyn Dodgers if you will reciprocate with a few cheers for The Spurs!

MEGAN *stares at him, pretending not to understand.* FRANK *turns and speaks to her as though deaf.*

The Tottenham Hotspur Football Club to the uninitiated!

MEGAN *bangs down the mug on the desk and breaks up to* BILL. FRANK *takes a small bottle from his waistcoat and shakes out a pill.*

Who are at present languishing next to the bottom of the League. However, the season does not finish until next April, so they have plenty of time to get themselves out of the mess.

Nora and all here join me in sending our best wishes for Christmas and the New Year. Sincerely, Frank.

He puts the pill in his mouth and takes a sip of water.

MEGAN *is moving slowly down towards centre table.*

HELENE *Will you tell Megan Wells she is out of her cotton-picking mind?*

MEGAN, *taken by surprise, reacts.* FRANK *smiles.*

If she's that bored with civilisation, why doesn't she just move to a Siberian salt mine?

MEGAN *sits upstage end of centre table and sorts books.*

South Africa? I can't even imagine it. But to tell the truth, I'm afraid of travelling... I'm not afraid of flying... I'm afraid of arriving. But I have been socking money away in the savings bank for next summer. If TV keeps feeding me, then I'm finally coming over!

As she types, HELENE *starts to sing "OVER THERE!".*
MEGAN *and* BILL *pick it up, and* FRANK *whistles the
tune. All are delighted at the news. In rhythm to the
tune,* MEGAN *is picking up books, building a pile up to
her chin. Suddenly* HELENE *ceases on "the drums are..."*

All freeze.

FRANK   March 16th 1956.

Dear Helene, we are still waiting to hear whether you are
finally coming to England this summer.

Freeze. Waiting. FRANK *looks at the* OTHERS. *Then back
front. A sense of urgency. All looking front.*

Both the girls are away at school, so you will have your
choice of beds at 37 Oakfield Court.

Freeze still held. All wait.

HELENE *doesn't know what to say.*

HELENE *(very quickly)* June 1st, 1956.

Dear Frank, Brian introduced me to Kenneth Graham's
Wind in the Willows and I have to have this. With the
Shephard illustrations, please, but *don't mail it – just
hold it for me till September...*

MEGAN *and* BILL *look at each other: this is it! She is
coming over in September! They cry out.* MEGAN *rushes
to embrace* FRANK.

And then mail it to the new address below.

HELENE *breaks down, crying.*

Those in the shop are stunned. FRANK *moves downstage
left, unable to believe it. The* OTHERS *watch him. He
goes to his desk. He closes the register and puts it inside
the desk. He looks at the duck and then puts that inside*

as well. He is 'burying' his pain and disappointment. He crosses to the shop door and steps outside. **MEGAN** *and* **BILL** *watch anxiously. All this is spaced out over the next lines.*

HELENE *rises.*

The sky fell on us in this cosy brownstone. We got eviction notices last month. They're renovating the building. I decided the time had come to get me a real apartment with real furniture...

She places scripts, books, etc. in a large cardboard box.

and in my right mind and shaking all over I went round to the construction site of a new building going up over on Second Avenue and signed a lease on a two-and-a-half (bed sitter) that isn't even there yet. I am now racing around buying furniture and bookshelves and wall-to-wall carpeting with all my English money!

But all my life I've been stuck in dilapidated furnished rooms and cockroach-y kitchens and I want to live like a lady, even if it means putting off England till it's paid for.

FRANK *now returns.* **HELENE** *starts to move the desk to what will be its new position. Also the desk chair.*

Meanwhile the landlord thinks we are not moving out fast enough and is encouraging us by firing the super, leaving nobody to give us hot water or take the garbage out, and also by ripping out the mailboxes, the hall-light fixtures and – as of this week – the wall between my kitchen and bathroom. All this and the Dodgers disintegrating before my very eyes, nobody knows the trouble I see!

She exits.

Lights change to autumnal glow. We hear a phrase from the spiritual 'NOBODY KNOWS THE TROUBLE I SEEN'.

BILL, *at his desk, anxiously watches* **FRANK,** *but drops his gaze and goes on working when* **FRANK** *returns.*

FRANK *takes out a pipe and strikes a match.*

May 3rd 1956. *(he pauses, amazed)* Prepare yourself for a shock. All the books you require in your last letter are on the way to you and should arrive in a week or so. Don't ask us how we managed it – it's all part of the Marks & Co service!

Two of your friends dropped in to see us a few days ago and now I have forgotten their names. Unfortunately they had only time to stop and smoke a cigarette, as they were off again on their travels next morning.

He shuts the door and moves to the crate.

We seem to have had more American visitors than ever this year, including hundreds of lawyers, who march around with a large card pinned to their clothes, stating their hometown and name.

He lifts the crate and carries it to front of desk. **BILL,** *seeing this, shakes his head, then settles to work.*

They all seem to be enjoying their trip so you will have to make it next year. With all good wishes from us all, Frank.

He puts his pipe in his mouth, goes to the crate and stoops, looking for a book, finds it, and stands reading it.

Music cue: "NEW YORK, NEW YORK". **HELENE***'s set revolves to a new apartment. She enters with brightly coloured scatter cushions, a potted plant and Nora's Christmas card.*

HELENE January 10th 1958.

Apartment 15 c. 305 East 72nd Street, New York 21, New York.

Hey, Frankie, tell Nora to bring her address book up to date. Your Christmas card just got here; she sent it to the old address.

In your catalogue there's a list of *MacDonald Illustrated Classics*, which includes the *Essays of Elia*. I'd love to have this. If it's reasonable, of course. Nothing's cheap anymore.

She is now unpacking, hangs pictures, etc.

It's reasonable. Or "sensibly priced". There's a building going up over the street, the sign over it says "One and two bedroom apartments at Rents That Make Sense". Rents do *not* make sense. And prices do not sit around being reasonable.

FRANK *is sorting out books on the shelves.*

I go through life watching the English language being raped.

Whatever became of Plato's *Minor Dialogues*?

She exits.

FRANK *lowers the lid of the crate.*

FRANK Dear Helene, I must apologise for taking so long to answer your last letter but we have had rather a hectic time. Nora has been in hospital for the past several months and I have had my hands full at home. She is almost fully recovered and will be coming home in a week or so.

He sits on the crate. **BILL** *rises and crosses to the table to check something.*

It has been a trying time for us but, thanks to our National Health Service, it hasn't cost us a penny.

I don't know how to break the bad news but two days after offering you the *Shorter Oxford Dictionary* for your friend, a man came in and bought it when my back was turned.

He looks at **BILL,** *who shrugs apologetically.* **BILL** *moves away to a pile of books.*

I have delayed replying to your letter in the hope that another would come along but no luck yet. I am terribly sorry to disappoint your friend but you can blame it on me, as I really ought to have reserved it.

He looks at BILL, *who smiles. There is a pause.* BILL *moves upstage.* FRANK *rises and moves centre stage.*

About the *MacDonald Classics*, we do get a few from time to time but have none at the moment. We had several copies of – Lamb's *Essays of...*oh, um...*Elia*! – earlier on but they were snapped up during the holiday rush.

I am off on a buying trip next week and will look out for one for you.

He picks up a mug from his desk.

Not forgetting the Plato. We are all sorry to hear that your television shows have moved to Hollywood and that one more summer will bring us every American tourist but the one we want to see. I can quite understand your refusal to leave New York for *Southern California.*

We have our fingers crossed for you and hope that some sort of work will turn up soon. Sincerely, Frank

He drinks the contents and then moves upstage with the mug. He stands by BILL.

HELENE *re-enters, and puts on a large man's dressing gown.*

HELENE Sir, I write to say I have got work.

FRANK *sits left of centre table. He looks up at this news.* BILL *rises, takes his mug and exits.*

I won it, I won a 5,000-dollar grant off CBS. It's supposed to support me for a year while I write American history dramatisations.

FRANK *turns to listen.*

I'm starting with a script about New York under seven years of British occupation and I *marvel* how I rise above it to address you in a friendly and forgiving fashion, your behaviour over here from 1776 to 1783 was simply *filthy*. Is there any such thing as a modern version of the *Canterbury Tales*? I have these guilts about never having read Chaucer. Love to Nora. Anything she needs, let me know.

Sound of a siren. She puts on her spectacles and settles to work.

The interior of the shop is now wintry.

FRANK Dear Helene, thank you very much for your kind offer but there really is nothing we need. We are delighted to hear that you have won a grant and are working again. We are prepared to be broad-minded about your choice of subject matter, but I must tell you *(looking at* **BILL***)* that one of the young inmates here confessed that until he read your letter he never knew that England had ever owned the States.

HELENE *reacts to the above.*

Very softly some Corelli is heard. Outside the shop it is now snowing. **FRANK** *sits at the work table upstage.* **HELENE** *rises and pours herself a gin.*

HELENE *has been drinking too much gin. The scene that follows goes at quite a speed, building to a crescendo, part despair, part the clown, hiding her loneliness.*

HELENE Sunday night and a hell of a way to start 1960. I don't know, Frankie.

FRANK *feels the cold, blows on his hands. Then rises and moves to the shop window, watching the snow. He puts on a scarf and overcoat. He gets out his pipe and matches.*

HELENE *lifts an enormous book off the floor.*

Somebody gave me this book for Christmas. It's a Giant
Modern Library book. Did you ever see one of those? *(carries
book to desk)* It's less attractively bound than the *Proceedings
of the New York Assembly* and it weighs more. It was given
to me by a gent who knows I am fond of John Donne. The
title of this book is

The Complete Poetry

and

Selected Prose

of JOHN DONNE

and

The Complete Poetry

of

WILLIAM BLAKE?

The question mark is mine. Will you please tell me what
those two boys have in common, except they were both
English and they both wrote?

FRANK *moves upstage centre to chair at the work table
and leans against a chair, pipe in mouth, listening.*

I tried reading the Introduction, figuring that might explain
it. The Introduction is in four parts. Parts One and Two
include a professor's life of Donne *mit* illustrations from
the-author's-works-also-criticism. Part Three begins – and
God knows I quote "When, as a little boy, William Blake
saw the prophet Ezekiel under a tree amid a summer field,
he was soundly trounced by his mother!"

FRANK *sits centre stage.*

I mean, the back of the Lord God or the face of the Virgin
Mary, all right – but why the hell should anyone want to see
the prophet Ezekiel? I don't like Blake anyway, he swoons

too much. It's Donne I'm writing about. I am being driven clean up the wall. Frankie, you have got to help me.

FRANK *moves swiftly and sits in the chair at the table by the desk.* HELENE *sits on her swivel chair at her desk, legs over the arm rest.*

Here I was, curled up in my armchair so at peace with the world, with something old and serene on the radio – Corelli or somebody – and this thing on the table. This Giant Modern Library thing. So I thought, "I will read the three standard passages from *Sermon XV* aloud" – you have to read Donne aloud, it's like a Bach fugue. Would you like to know what I went through in an innocent attempt to read three contiguous uncut passages from *Sermon XV* out loud?

FRANK *strikes a match and lights his pipe.* HELENE *rises and relates the following speech to the books in question.*

OK, you start with the Giant Modern Library version, you locate *Sermon XV*, and there they are: Excerpts 1, 2 and 3 – only when you get to the end of Excerpt 1 you discover they have deleted Jezebel.

So you get down *Donne's Sermons: Selected Passages* (Logan Pearsall Smith), where you spend twenty minutes locating *Sermon XV*, Excerpt 1, because by Logan Pearsall Smith it isn't *Sermon XV*, Excerpt 1, it's Passage 126, *All Must Die.* Now that you've found it, you find he also deleted Jezebel.

So you get down the *Complete Poetry and Selected Prose* (Nonesuch Press), but they didn't happen to select Jezebel either. So you get down the *Oxford Book of English Prose*, where you spend another twenty minutes locating it, because in the *Oxford English Prose* it isn't *Sermon XV*, Excerpt 1, nor yet 126, *All Must Die*, it's Passage 113, *Death the Leveller.* Jezebel is there! And you read it aloud, but when you get to the end of it, you find it doesn't have either Excerpt 2 or 3 so you switch to one of the other three books – provided you had the wit to leave all three open in the right pages, which I didn't! So – break it to me gently: how hard is it going to be to find me John Donne's *Complete Sermons*, and how much is it going to cost?

FRANK *makes a face. Midnight begins to strike in New York. Sound of car hooters, crackers, fireworks, voices shouting "Happy new year!" All the bells of New York begin to ring.*

HELENE *picks up the now nearly empty gin bottle.*

Happy new year!!! Yours, H. Hanf – f-f-f-f!

She exits.

FRANK *softly claps his hands.*

Sound out and light change.

It is now spring.

Enter **BILL** *in trilby hat and a smart suit, carrying a rolled up umbrella.* **BILL** *stands at his table, sorting mail. He takes out a pair of horn-rimmed spectacles to do this. His hair is fuller now, styles are changing.*

He hands some of the letters to **FRANK**.

FRANK March 5th 1960.

Dear Helene, I have delayed answering your last two letters until I had some good news to report.

He rises

I have managed to obtain a copy of the Bernard Shaw–Ellen Terry correspondence. It is not a very attractive edition but it is a good clean copy and I thought I had better send it as this is quite a popular book and it might be some time before another copy comes along. The price is approximately...? Oh, dear...

BILL Two dollars eighty-five!

FRANK Two dollars eighty-five! And you have a credit with us of twenty-five cents.

He rings the bell and **THOMAS,** *the new assistant, enters brightly.* **FRANK** *stares at him, bemused, then hands him the book and the boy exits.* **BILL** *follows* **THOMAS** *to check he knows what to do.*

BILL Thomas!

FRANK I'm afraid the complete Donne *Sermons* can be had only by buying Donne's *Complete Works.* This runs to more than forty volumes and would be very expensive if in good condition.

He leans forward on his desk, yawns, removes spectacles. His pipe is in his left hand.

We hope you had a good Christmas and New Year, in spite of Jezebel and the Giant Modern Library. Nora joins me in sending best wishes. Sincerely, Frank.

He falls asleep during the next speech.

HELENE *enters with the book and letter.*

HELENE Monsieur de Tocqueville's compliments and he begs to announce his safe arrival in America. It's a beautiful book and you can't even call it second-hand, the pages weren't cut.

She puts the book down on the desk and takes a paper knife to open the letter.

Did I tell you I finally found the perfect page-cutter? It's a pearl-handled fruit knife. My mother left me a dozen of them. I keep one in the pencil cup on my desk. Maybe I go with the wrong kind of people, but I'm just not likely to have twelve guests all sitting round simultaneously eating fruit.

She has now opened the letter and a cheque flutters out.

Frank! Frank, you still there?

She sits with the letter, stunned.

You won't believe this. I sold a story to *Harper's Magazine* – slaved over it for three weeks and they paid me 200 dollars for it.

She lifts the letter.

Now they've got me writing the story of my life! They're advancing me 1,500 dollars to write it,

And they figure it shouldn't take me more than six months! So I can't buy any books, much less travel to London, but back in October somebody introduced me to Louis, the Duke of Saint-Simon, in a miserable abridgement and I tore round to the Society Library and got the real thing. And last night I realised I could not support the notion that when I take it back I will have *no* Louis in the house.

She puts cheque away and rises.

I'll settle for any edition you can find that you trust. *Do not mail it!* Just buy it, let me know what it costs and I'll buy it from you one volume at a time. Hope Nora and the girls are fine. And anybody else who knows me. Helene.

She exits.

FRANK *wakes up and his pipe falls to the ground. He wipes rheum from his eyes and puts on his spectacles. He moves to front of desk and picks up his pipe. As though to make up for falling asleep on the job, he now moves swiftly – still absent-mindedly in his overcoat – to centre table for the six volumes of Saint-Simon.*

FRANK Dear Helene, you will be pleased to know that we have a copy of the *Memoirs of the Duke de Saint-Simon* in stock, six volumes nicely bound and in very good condition.

He moves upstage with the books.

We are sending them off to you today and they should arrive within a week or two. The amount due on them is approximately eighteen dollars seventy-five but don't worry about paying it all at once.

He rings the bell and THOMAS *enters.* FRANK *moves away, holding the books. He has forgotten he rang for the boy.* THOMAS *follows him.*

Your credit will always be good at Marks and Company. It was very good to hear from you again. We are all well and still hoping to see you in England one of these days. Love from us all.

He turns and sees THOMAS *who gestures towards the books.* FRANK *gives them to him and he exits to pack them.* FRANK *sits at the table right of desk, checking accounts in ledger.*

HELENE *re-enters.*

HELENE March 10th 1961.

Dear Frankie, Enclosed please God, please find a ten-dollar bill. It better get there, not many of those float in here these days, but Louis wanted me to get him paid off. I'm having trouble with my bank. Nothing infuriates me like those friendly folksy ads in magazines and on TV. Every bank I ever walked into was about as folksy as a cobra.

Frankie, I'm gloomy. I just read a casual description of London by Hazlitt – I had to put the book down, suddenly engulfed in a wave of longing that was like homesickness.

I wanted to see London the way old people want to see home before they die. And Oxford. I have to see Trinity College, where John Donne, John Henry Newman and Arthur Quiller-Couch all lived in their various long-gone eras. Whatever I know about writing English, those three men taught me, and before I die I want to stand in their freshmen's rooms and call their names blessed.

She sits on cushions at the very edge of her platform,
and very close to FRANK.

I thought of you last night. My editor from Harper's was here for dinner. We were going over the story of my life and we came to how I dramatised Landor's *Aesop and Rhodope* for the *Hallmark Hall of Fame*. We were going over this anecdote and Gene – my editor – said, "Who is Landor?" and I plunged into an enthusiastic explanation and Gene shook her head and cut in impatiently, "You and your Olde English Books!"

You see how it is, Frankie?

FRANK Mmmm!

HELENE You're the only soul alive who understands me.

The Beatles's "YESTERDAY" starts to be heard. They both
hear the music.

From outside the shop comes the sound of the Beatles
song. FRANK *looks up, rises, goes to the door and opens*
it. It reminds him of something – yes, the Easter duck!
He opens his desk and brings it out, and starts talking
to it directly as he sets it once again on his desk.

FRANK October 14th 1963.

Dear Helene! You will be surprised to learn that the two volumes of Virginia Woolf's *Common Reader* are on their way to you.

If you want anything else, I can probably get it for you with the same efficiency and swiftness!

He finds the two green volumes of Virginia Woolf in a
cardboard box. As he straightens up, he has a twinge.
Slowly straightening, he rings the bell.

We are all jogging along as usual. My elder daughter Sheila – twenty-four – suddenly decided she wanted to be

a teacher, so she threw up her secretarial job two years ago
to go to college.

He rings the bell a second time.

She has another year to go, so it looks as though it will be
a long time before our children will be able to keep us in
luxury.

THOMAS *enters for books.*

Love from us all here, Frank.

Music out. **FRANK** *crosses to the crate to find the Chaucer.
He rummages inside it.*

Oh, P.S. Some time ago you asked me for a modern version of
Chaucer's *Canterbury Tales.* I came across a little volume the
other day which I thought you would like. It is not complete
by any means but it is quite a cheap book. I am sending it
along by book post. It appears to be quite a scholarly edition.
If this whets your appetite for Chaucer, *(holds book up)* let
me know and I will see what I can find.

HELENE *(holding an identical copy of the Chaucer)* All
right, that's enough Chaucer made easy!

She throws it in her bin, bang!

Simultaneously **FRANK** *drops his copy into the crate,
bang! And slams lid, bang!*

I'm glad I read it. I liked reading about the nun who ate so
dainty she never dripped any grease on herself. I've never
been able to make that claim and I use a fork.

*She sits on sofa, picks up a gin bottle which is on the
floor, and pours a drink.* **FRANK** *moves to his desk and,
opening a ledger, makes entries, his pipe in one hand.*

Wasn't anything else that interested me much, it's just
stories... Now, if Chaucer had kept a diary and told me

what it was like to be a clerk in the palace of Richard II, *that* I'd learn Olde English for. It was just some slob's version of what it was like to live in the time of Oliver Cromwell – only the slob didn't *live* in the time of Oliver Cromwell, so how the hell does he know what it was like? Anybody who wants to know what it was like to live in the time of Oliver Cromwell can flop on the sofa with Milton on his pro side and Walton on his con, and they'll not tell him what it was like, they'll take him there. "The reader will not credit that such things could be", Walton says somewhere or other, "but I was there and I saw it".

She picks up the bottle, glass and book, and is about to go on working.

That's for me. I'm a great lover of I-was-there books!

BILL *enters down the stairs.*

I enclose two bucks for the Virginia Woolf and that leaves me with a credit with you of sixty-five cents, which is a larger credit than I have anywhere else.

BILL *rings the bell.*

Do you ever hear anything of Cecily or Megan?

Enter **MRS TODD**. **BILL** *talks to her.* **THOMAS** *follows with the trolley and they start to clear books.* **THOMAS** *exits with the first load.* **FRANK** *is still in his overcoat and scarf.* **BILL** *crosses to him with the post, which includes a quilted envelope containing the E.M. Delderfield.*

FRANK Dear Helene, it was good to hear from you again. We have not heard from Cecily Farr in some years now. Megan Wells had enough of South Africa in a very short time and did stop in to give us a chance to say I-told-you-so before going out to try her luck in Australia. We had a Christmas card from her a few years ago but nothing recently.

Sorting the mail, he finds the package and opens it.

I've just managed to obtain a copy of E.M. Delderfield's *Diary of a Provincial Lady* and am sending it off to you today.

He holds out the book. MRS TODD *takes it from him and rings the bell for* THOMAS, *who re-enters.* FRANK *moves down centre.*

We had a very pleasant summer with more than the usual number of tourists, including hordes of young people making the pilgrimage to Carnaby Street.

BILL *checks his watch: time for his lunch break. He closes his file and crosses to get his hat and umbrella.*

We watch it all from a safe distance, though I must say I rather like the Beatles.

BILL *is at the door and he and* FRANK *exchange a smile.* MRS TODD *and* THOMAS *also smile.*

If their fans just wouldn't scream so!

BILL *exits whistling, or singing, "YESTERDAY".*

HELENE *lifts the box and exits.*

Yes, we're still here, getting older and busier, but no richer.

MRS TODD *and* THOMAS *exit.*

Nora and the girls send their love, Frank.

He moves down to the crate to fill it with books lying on the floor. The crate has a false bottom so it will be only half full when he comes to lift it.

HELENE *enters in a long housecoat, which will conceal her final costume. Her hair is greyer.*

HELENE September 30th. 19...68!

Still alive, are we?

She picks up a cardboard box and starts to pack textbooks. FRANK is on his knees downstage, also packing books into the crate.

I've been writing American history books for children for four or five years. Got hung up on the stuff and have been buying American history books – in ugly, cardboard-y American editions. Somehow I just didn't think the stately homes of England would yield nice English editions of James Madison's stenographic record of the Constitutional Convention, or Thomas Jefferson's letters to John Adams, or like that. Are you a grandfather yet?

FRANK, pipe in mouth, looks up.

Tell Sheila and Mary their children are entitled to presentation copies of my *Collected Juvenile Works... that* should make them rush off and reproduce.

FRANK smiles.

HELENE lifts the box.

I introduced a young friend of mine to *Pride and Prejudice* one rainy Sunday and she has gone out of her mind for Jane Austen. She has a birthday around Hallowe'en, can you find me some Austen for her? If you've got a complete set, let me know the price; if it's expensive, I'll make her husband give her half and I'll give her half. Best to Nora and everybody else around, Helene

She carries the box into her hall, then returns to her desk, sips gin, picks up the Newman, caresses it, then returns to her notes.

During the next speech, FRANK closes the lid of the crate, lifts it – as though it's very heavy – and carries it towards centre stage, but has to drop it on the floor. Once again it is snowing outside.

FRANK Dear Helene, Yes, we are all very much alive and kicking, though rather exhausted from a hectic summer with hordes of tourists from the USA, France, Scandinavia, etc. all buying our nice leather-bound books. Consequently our stock at the moment is a sorry sight, and with the shortage of books and high prices, there is little hope of finding any Jane Austen for you in time for your friend's birthday. Perhaps we will be able to find them for her for Christmas.

He lowers the crate. Bent over, he slowly straightens. He senses something has happened... He leaves the crate. He decides to go home. He will collect the hat, briefcase and umbrella.

Nora and the girls are fine. Sheila is teaching. Mary is engaged to a very nice boy, but there is little hope of them getting married for some time as neither has any money! So Nora's hopes of being a glamorous grandmother are receding fast!

He has now opened the door, pauses to look round the shop.

Love, Frank.

He exits.

Enter briskly from outer office **MRS TODD** *with a file. She crosses to* **FRANK***'s desk and puts the duck inside.*

MRS TODD 8th January 1969.

Dear Miss Hanff...

HELENE *looks up.*

I have just come across the letter you wrote to Mr Doel on the 30th of September last, and it is with great regret that I have to tell you that he passed away on Sunday the 22nd of December. The funeral took place last week. He was rushed to hospital and operated on at once for a ruptured appendix. Unfortunately peritonitis set in and he died seven days later.

On the last three words she slowly closes the ledger and exits. Lights will slowly fade to blackout, leaving light only on **HELENE** *who holds the letter, but knows its contents by heart.*

HELENE He had been with the firm for over forty years and naturally it has come as a very great shock to Mr Cohen, particularly coming so soon after the death of Mr Marks. He is left with no alternative but to close the shop.

Yours faithfully, Joan Todd – for Marks and Company.

In the darkened shop, the shelves in the windows swivel and become filled with copies of the Andre Deutsch edition of 84 Charing Cross Road.

Sound of a jet plane.

Lights fade on **HELENE,** *who is in tears.*

In the blackout, she exits to change.

And under cover of the plane noise the bookshelves in the shop slide away to reveal empty shelves when the lights come up.

The **PILOT**'s *announcement covers this, also giving* **HELENE** *time to get round to the other side of the stage.*

Once the shelves are clear, lights come up slowly on the shop. It really should be a cross-fade because if there is a total blackout the audience is likely to applaud, thinking this is the end!

PILOT *(recorded)* Ladies and gentlemen, this is the Captain speaking. We will be landing at Heathrow Airport in approximately ten minutes. Would you kindly fasten your seat belts, bring your seats to the upright positions, and observe the non-smoking signs. We hope that you enjoyed your flight and that you will fly with us again. Thank you.

Plane is heard disappearing into the distance.

We see HELENE *in a blue trouser suit, blue handbag over her shoulder, a red-white-and-blue silk scarf knotted round her neck, and holding a copy of her book. As she opens the door, music ceases and she enters the shop in silence, as she gazes around at the empty shelves. She removes her spectacles and speaks.*

HELENE Theoretically it was one of the happiest days of my life. Year after year I had planned a pilgrimage, only to have it cancelled at the last minute by some crisis, usually financial. This time it was different. I'd written a book called *84 Charing Cross Road* and a few months after it came out in New York in 1971, a London publisher, named Andre Deutsch, bought it for publication in England. He wrote me that the London edition would be brought out in June and he wanted me here to help publicise the book.

She moves towards FRANK's *desk.*

It had felt unreal knowing I was on my way to that address. I'd bought books from here for twenty years. I'd made friends here whom I never met. Most of the books I bought from Marks and Company were probably available in New York, but I'd wanted a link with London and I'd managed it. *(pause)* How about this, Frankie? I finally made it.

Music of "KNIGHTSBRIDGE", *from Coates's* "LONDON SUITE", *starts softly and builds and will play fortissimo through the curtain calls.*

The End

FURNITURE AND PROPERTY LIST

HELENE'S APARTMENT

Bookcases
Pin board for cards, mementoes and cuttings
Postcards
Shakespeare bust
Piccadilly Circus sign
Hook
Oval rug
Desk. On it: typewriter, pile of typing paper, in tray, scripts, stationery pot (containing pens, pencils, scissors and letter opener), pens and pencils (fountain pen, pencils and red pencil), letter rack, pencil sharpener, ashtray, cigarette packet, lighter, notepad, airmail envelopes
Mounds of catalogues, old torn books, ephemera
Orange crate bookshelves
Wastepaper basket
Swivel chair
Sofa: handbag, purse and six dollars
Box for posting letters

BOOKSHOP

Bookcases and books
Desk. On it: order book, old-fashioned telephone, work lamp, cash box, English notes and coins, fountain pen, letter opener, ledger, bell, pile of headed paper, blotter
Wastepaper basket
Chair
Stepladder
Large table
Chairs
Books
Scissors
Fountain pen
Small table (next to **Frank**'s desk)
Frank's desk. On it: fountain pen, letter opener, ledger, letter rack, pen pot, book ends
Stool

Wastepaper basket
Hat stand
Small bookcase with doors
Plan chest/portfolio shelves
"Open/closed" sign on door
Publisher's logo
Prints clipped to a string across the door
Curtains for shop windows
Pendant lights (for shop windows)
Small and large ceiling light

ACT I

Invoice papers (**Mr Martin**)
Pile of post with Helene's letter on top (**Megan**) p.1
The Saturday Review of Literature, 1st October 1949 (**Helene**) p.3
Pencil (**Bill** - behind his ear)
Briefcase (**Mr Martin**)
Brown paper and string
Invoices x2 written on stage (**Megan**) p.7
Catalogue (**Frank**) p.8
British food company catalogue (**Helene**) p.8
Extra catalogues for **Helene** to go through p.8
Large wooden box
Custom labels for box p.9
Tins of pork sausages, tins of bacon, tins of cheese, tinned cake, packet of dried eggs and tins of jam p.9
Large tin of ham p.9
Small wooden box tied with string (**Mr Martin** and **Cecily**) p.11
Easter eggs in box, boxes of shelled eggs, absurd duck with label p.11
Umbrella, briefcase and hat (**Frank**) p.12
Letters and clipboard (**Cecily**) p.12
Spectacles (**Helene**) p.13
Woollen jacket (**Helene**) p.14
Invoices (**Mr Martin**)
Pile of letters (**Cecily**) p.14
Briefcase and umbrella (**Frank**) p.15
Two books, one wrapped in tissue paper (**Frank**) p.15
Snapshots (**Cecily**) p.17

Large pages from Clarendon Press, creased (**Helene**) p.19
Spectacles (**Frank**) p.20
Bell (**Megan**) p.20
Invoice (**Megan**) p.20
Crate p.21
Apron (**Helene**) p.21
Mug of coffee (**Helene**) p.22
Pile of mail (**Bill**) p.23
Small card found inside her small book (**Helene**) p.25/26
Coins and purse (**Maxine**) p.29
Invoice (**Cecily**) p.32
Crates with books inside (**Bill**) p.32
Trolley (**Bill**) p.32
Clipboard with checklist (**Megan**) p.32
Invoice (**Megan**) p.33
Bottle of Gin and glass (**Helene**) p.35
Paper hat (**Frank**) p.35
Glass of wine (**Frank**) p.35
Blowers/squeakers and paper hats (**Megan, Bill** and **Cecily**)
p.35
False nose (**Bill**) p.36
Mistletoe (**Bill**) p.36
Handkerchief (**Frank**) p.36
Large wrapped box (**Bill, Cecily** and **Megan**) p.36
Christmas label p.36
Christmas card p.37
Christmas box p.37
Tablecloth (**Helene**) p.38
TV scripts (**Helene**) p.39
Watch (**Cecily**) p.37
Keys p.40
Cups of coffee and saucers, tray, sugar bowl, spoon (**Cecily** and
Megan) p.41
Ukelele (**Bill**) p.44

ACT II

Bunting p.46
Cardboard box (**Helene**) p.46
Radio (**Helene**) p.48
Small round suitcase (**Cecily**) p.50

Thank you note (**Cecily**) p.50
Marks & Co catalogue (**Helene**) p.51
New York Times (**Helene**) p.51
Script (**Helene**) p.51
Watch (**Helene**) p.51
Briefcase (**Helene**) p.51
Cup of tea (**Bill**) p.53
Small pill bottle and pills (**Frank**) p.53
Large cardboard box (**Helene**) p.55
Pipe (**Frank**) p.56
Match (**Frank**) p.56
Crate (**Frank**) p.56
Brightly coloured cushions, a potted plant and Nora's Christmas
card (**Helene**) p.56
Pictures to hang (**Helene**) p.57
Umbrella (**Bill**) p.62
Mail (**Bill**) p.62
Horn-rimmed spectacles (**Bill**) p.62
Paper knife (**Helene**) p.63
Cheque (**Helene**) p.63
Ledger (**Frank**) p.65
Post (**Bill**) p.68
Quilted envelope (**Bill**) p.68
Crate (**Frank**) p.69
Textbooks (**Helene**) p.70
Glass of gin (**Helene**) p.70
File (**Mrs Todd**) p.71

SOUND/EFFECTS

Telephone rings (p.4)
Music of "JINGLE BELLS" (p.9)
Music swells (p.9)
Music out (p.9)
Sound of a New York siren (p.10)
Music for "EASTER PARADE" is heard (p.11)
Music swells (p.11)
Music swells (p.12)
Softly, from outside in the street, a barrel organ is heard (p.12)
Traffic noise, door closes, silence (p.12)
Music is now heard: the opening bars of Vaughan Williams's
"FANTASIA ON A THEME BY THOMAS TALLIS" (p.27)
Music out before she speaks (p.27)
The music of Eric Coates's "LONDON SUITE - KNIGHTSBRIDGE",
is heard (p.30)
Music still playing (p.31)
We hear the beginning of "FOR UNTO US A CHILD IS BORN" from
Handel's *Messiah* (p.35)
Music swells. From upstage centre a loud burst of squeakers
(p.35)
There is a loud burst of squeakers (p.35)
They laugh and blow squeakers again (p.36)
Blow their squeakers again (p.36)
Music out (p.36)
Sound of church bells (p.40)
We hear the honk of **Frank**'s car and the starting noises (p.44)
The curtain rises to the music of "ON THE TOWN" (p.46)
Music out (p.47)
We hear an excerpt from the radio broadcast of the coronation
(p.48)
We hear part of the BBC recording of the coronation of Queen
Elizabeth II, the section where John Snagge speaks of the
Queen Mother waiting to see her daughter present herself to her
people waiting outside the west door of Westminster Abbey, fol-
lowed by the fanfare, and then the whole congregation joining
in singing the national anthem (p.48)
Sound of New York church bells (p.51)
Sound of a siren (p.52)
We hear a phrase from the spiritual "NOBODY KNOWS THE

TROUBLE I SEEN" (p.56)
Music cue: *"NEW YORK, NEW YORK"* (p.56)
Sound of siren (p.59)
Very softly some Corelli is heard. Outside the shop it is now snowing (p.59)
Midnight begins to strike in New York. Sound of car hooters, crackers, fireworks, voices shouting "Happy new year!" All the bells of New York begin to ring (p.62)
Sound out (p.62)
The Beatles's *"YESTERDAY"* starts to be heard (p.66)
Music out (p.67)
Once again it is snowing outside (p.70)
In the darkened shop the shelves in the windows swivel and become filled with copies of the Andre Deutsch edition of *84 Charing Cross Road* (p.72)
Sound of a jet plane (p.72)
Plane heard disappearing into the distance (p72)
Music of *"KNIGHTSBRIDGE"*, from Coates's *"LONDON SUITE"* starts softly and builds and will play fortissimo through the curtain calls (p.73)

LIGHTING

The lights come up first on the shop (p.1)
Light change, spring 1950 (p.10)
Light change as though a storm is pending, sky darkening (p.27)
The shop is full of shadows (p.27)
Light changes to winter (p.35)
Major light change (p.48)
Wintry lighting (p.52)
Lights change to an autumnal glow (p.56)
The interior of the shop is now wintry (p.59)
Light change. It is now spring (p.62)
Lights will slowly fade to blackout, leaving light only on **Helene** (p.72)
Lights fade on **Helene** who is in tears (p.72)
In the blackout, she exits to change (p.72)
Once the shelves are clear – lights come up slowly on the shop. It really should be a cross-fade because if there is a total blackout the audience is likely to applaud (p.72)

CPSIA information can be obtained
at www.ICGtesting.com
Printed in the USA
BVHW090312300121
598883BV00008B/369

JUL   2021